Critters
A Greyscale Coloring Book

I have such an amazing Support System, Family, Friends and Fans of my photos and colorings, who all push me to create more books. I'd like to say....
Thank you All!

You can find me :

Facebook : @DigitalCreationsbyShawnBobar
Instagram : @digicreationsbyshawnbobar
Etsy : https://www.etsy.com/shop/DigiCreationsbyShawn

*The photos I have taken of house pets, I have been given permission to put their 'Critters' in my book.

Copyright © 2018 by Shawn Bobar
All photos property of Photography by Shawn M. Bobar
All Rights Reserved.

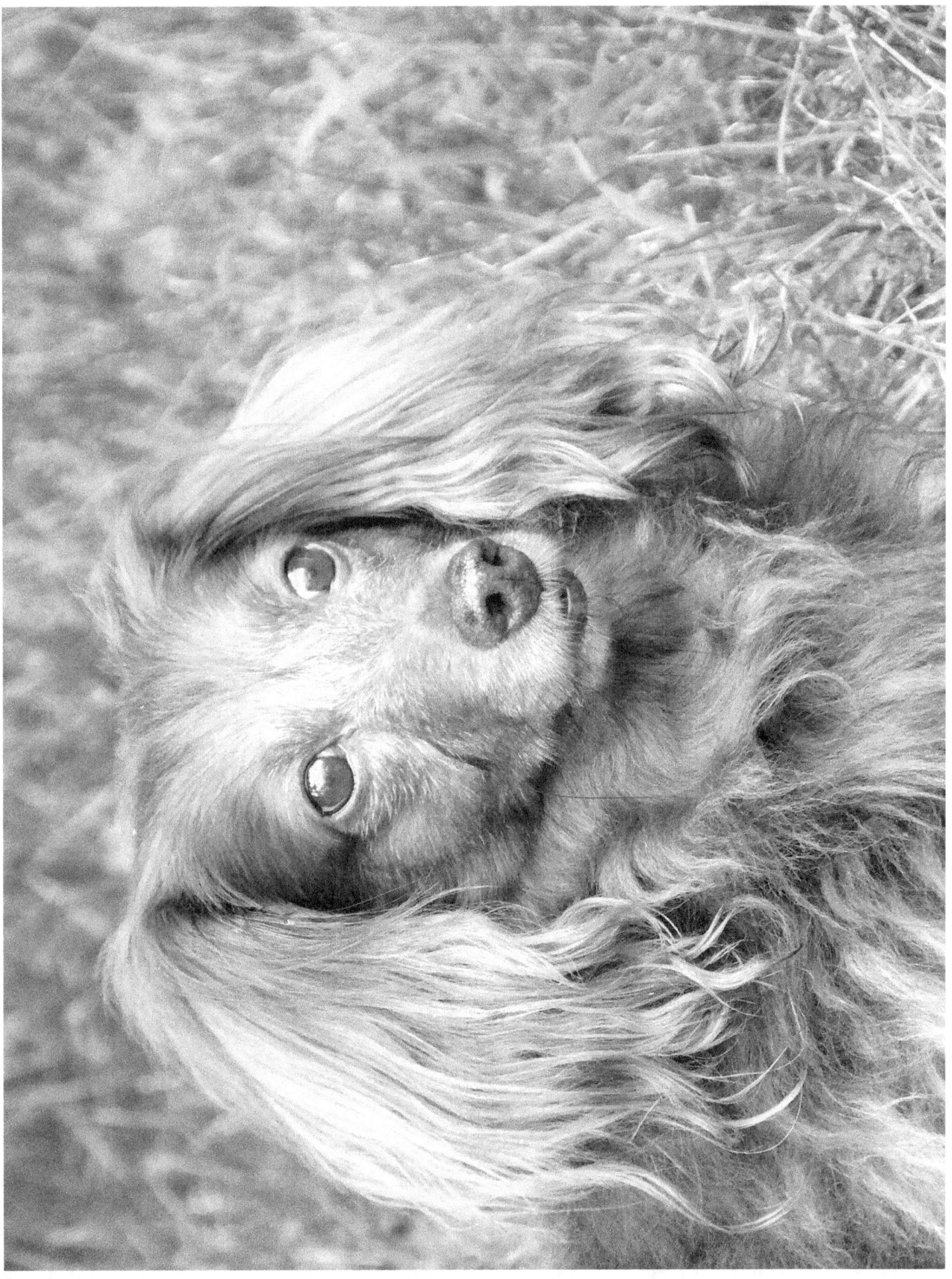

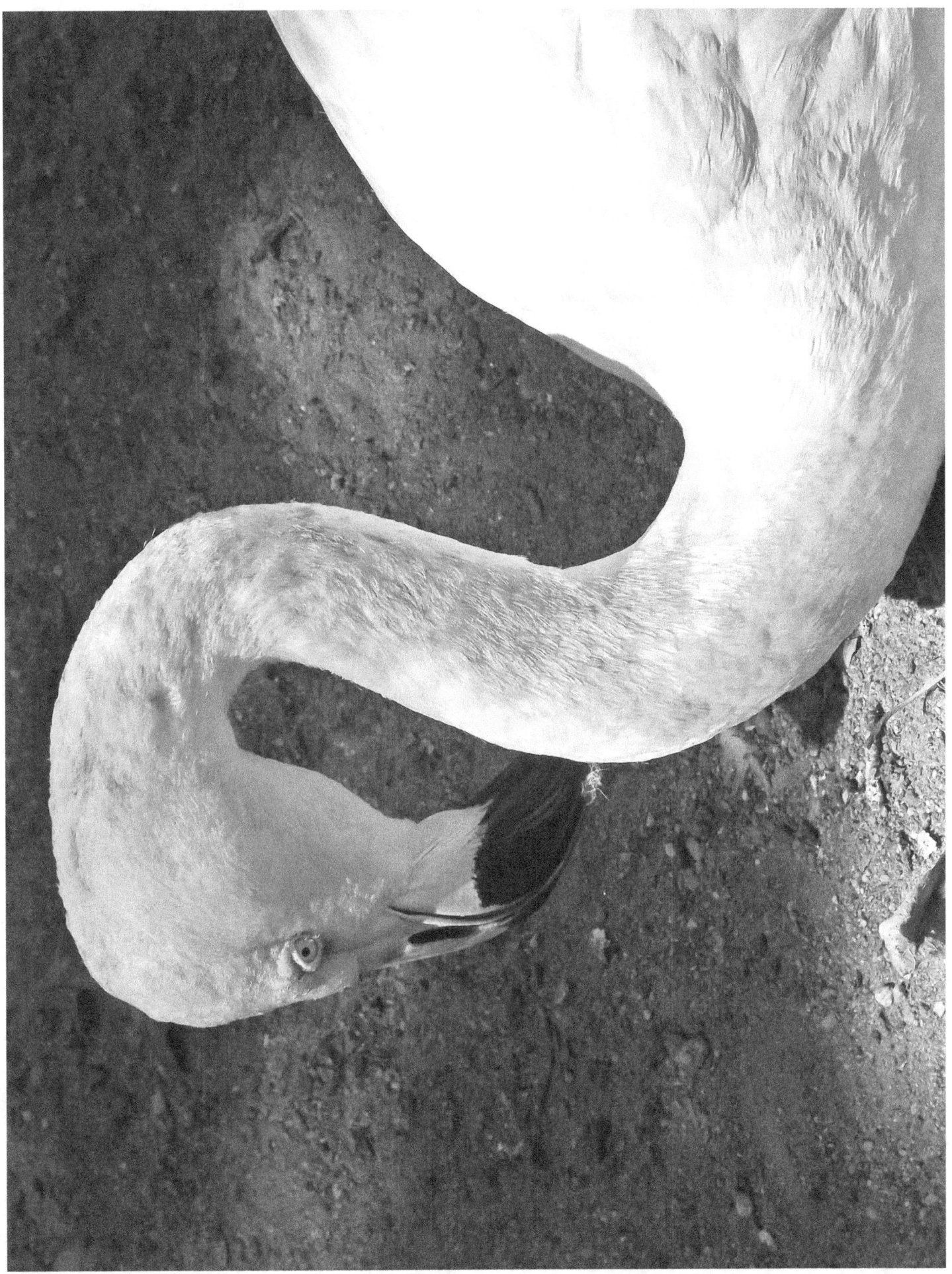

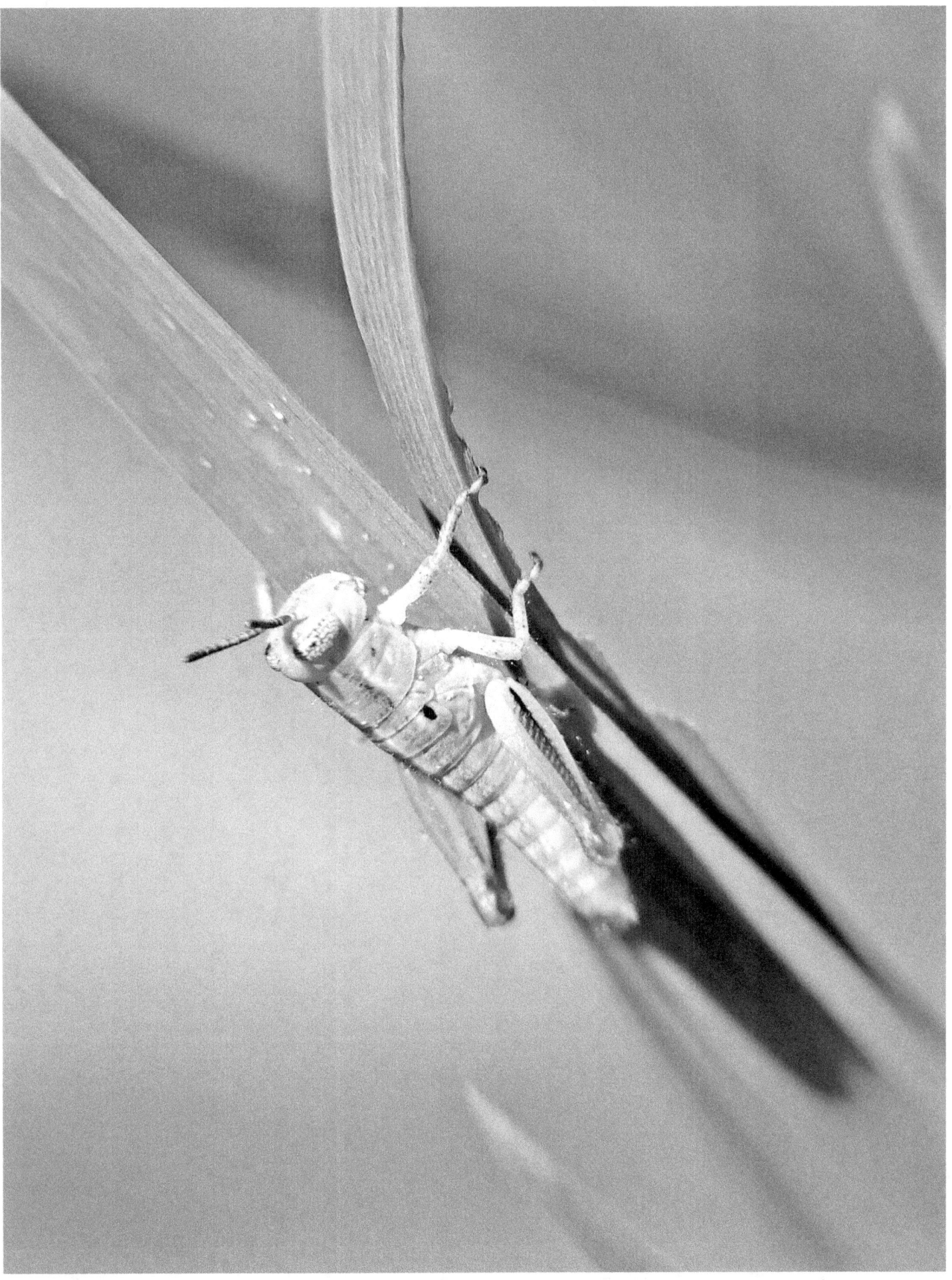

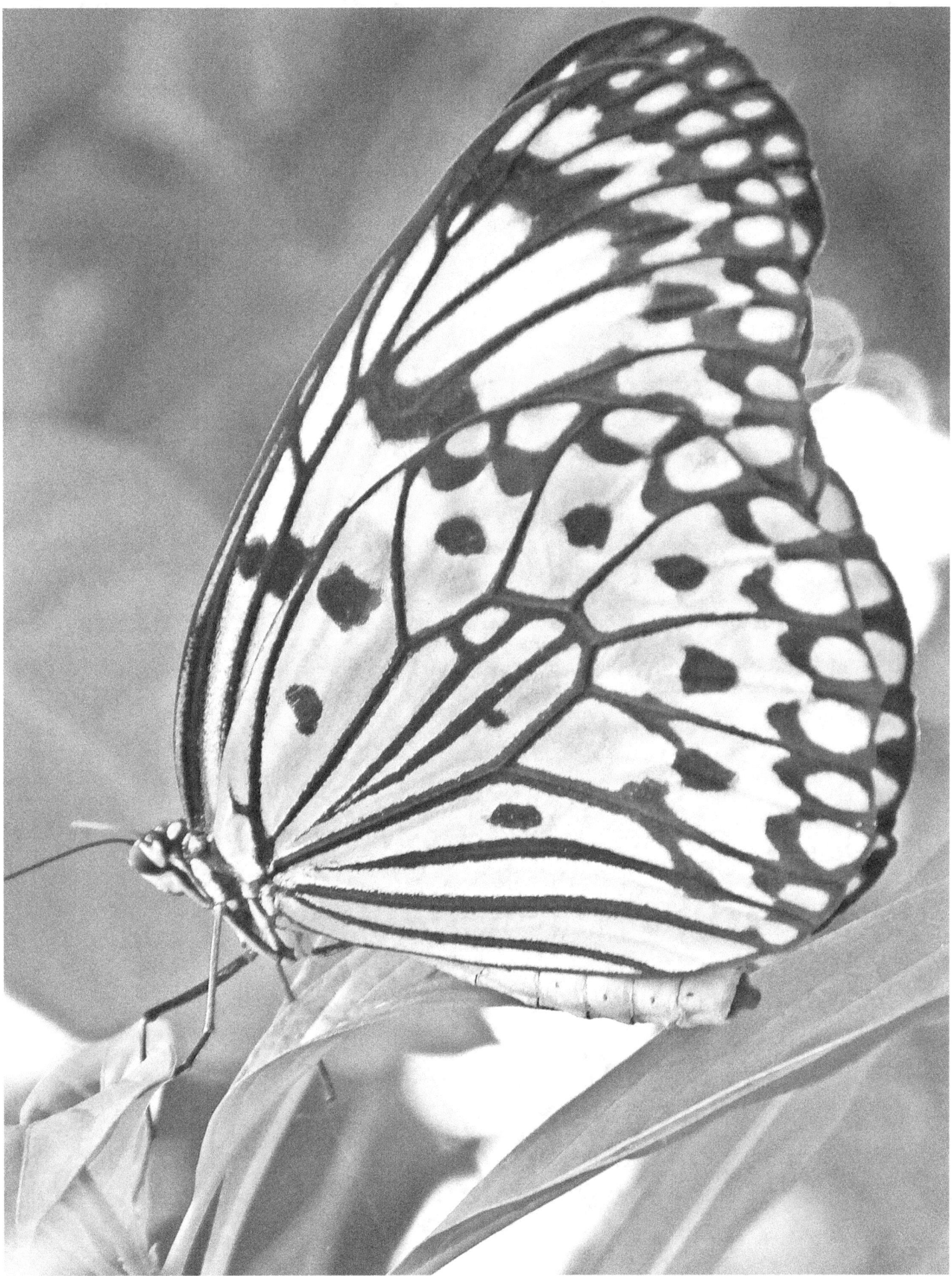

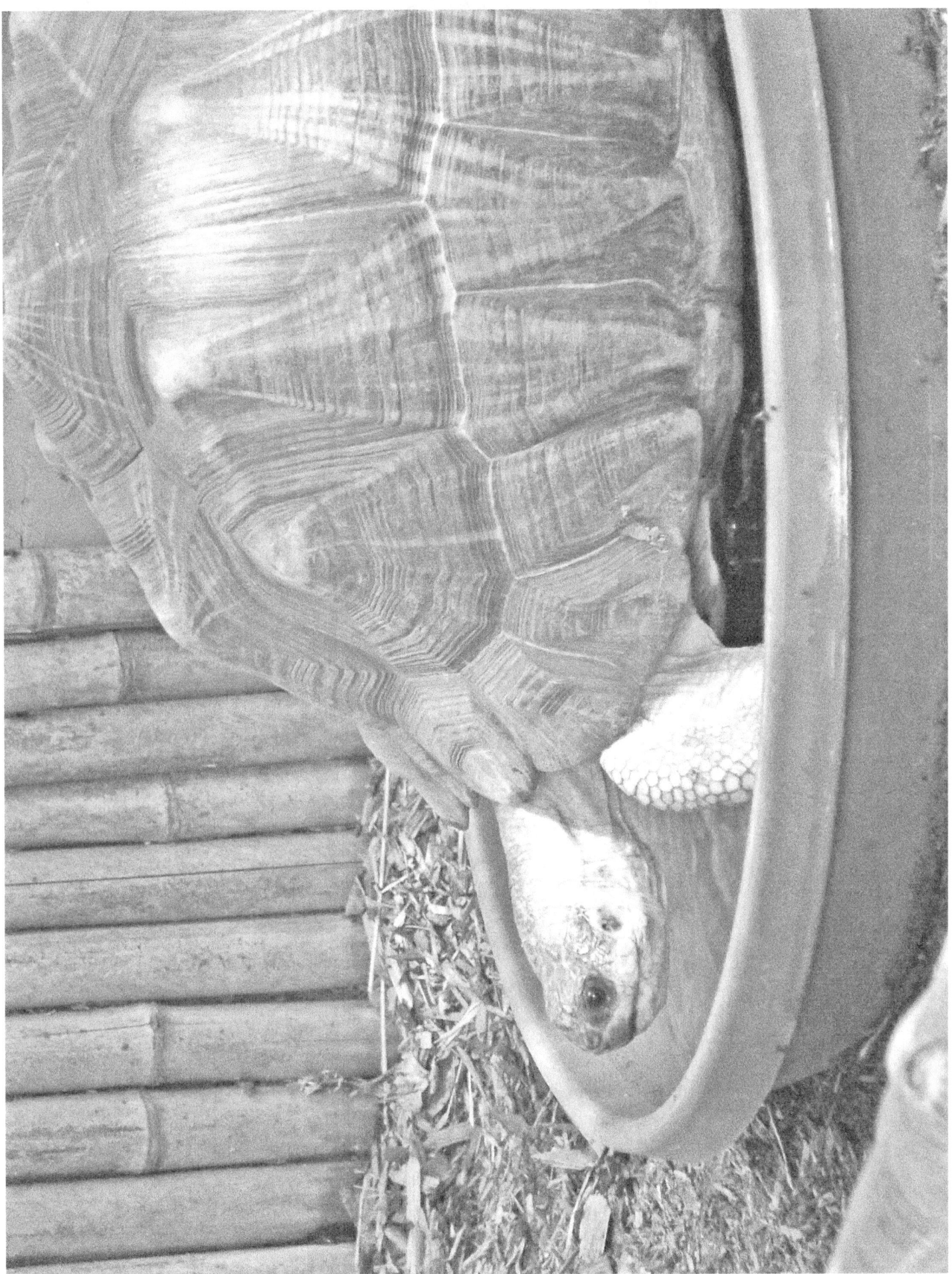

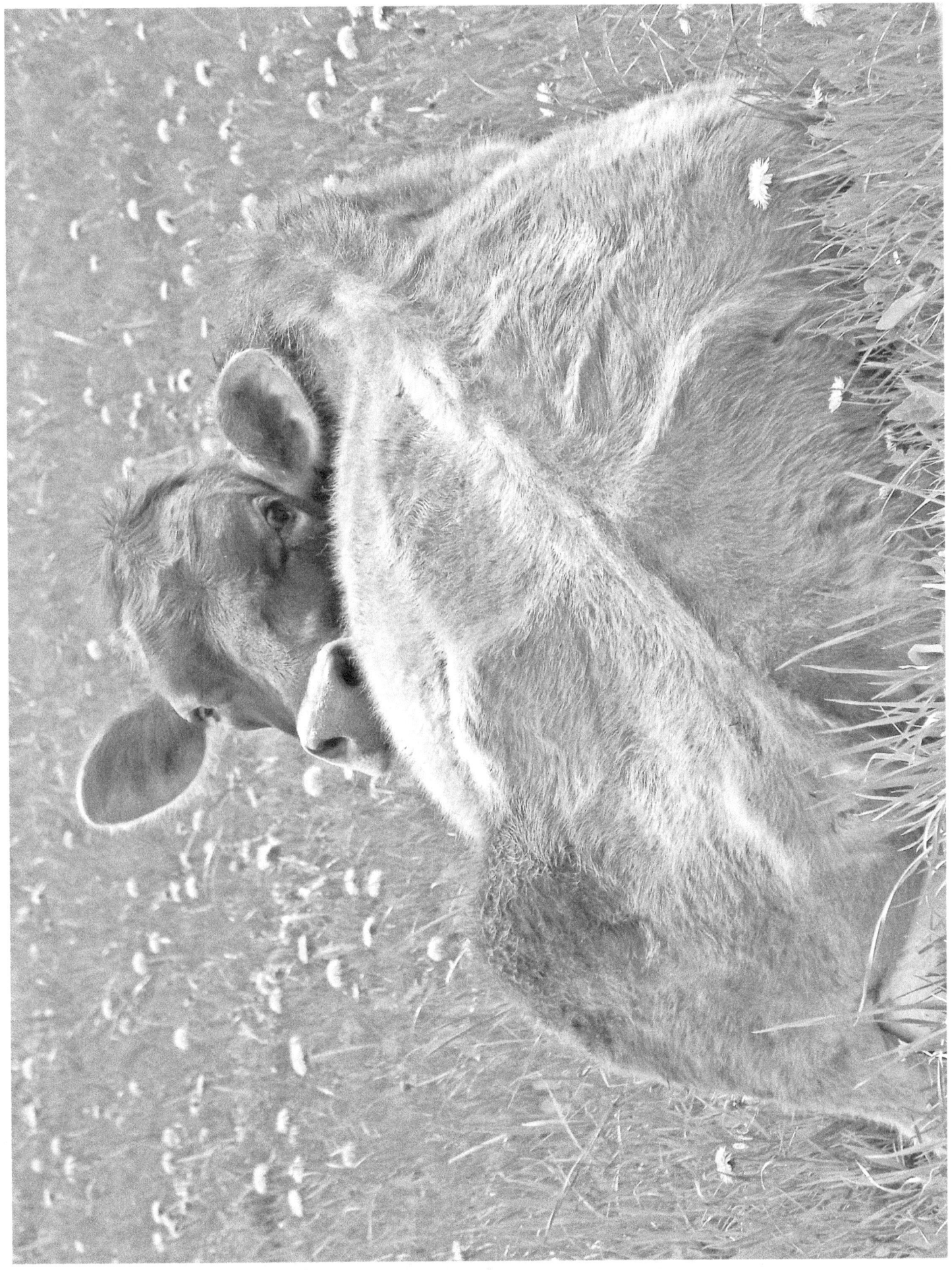

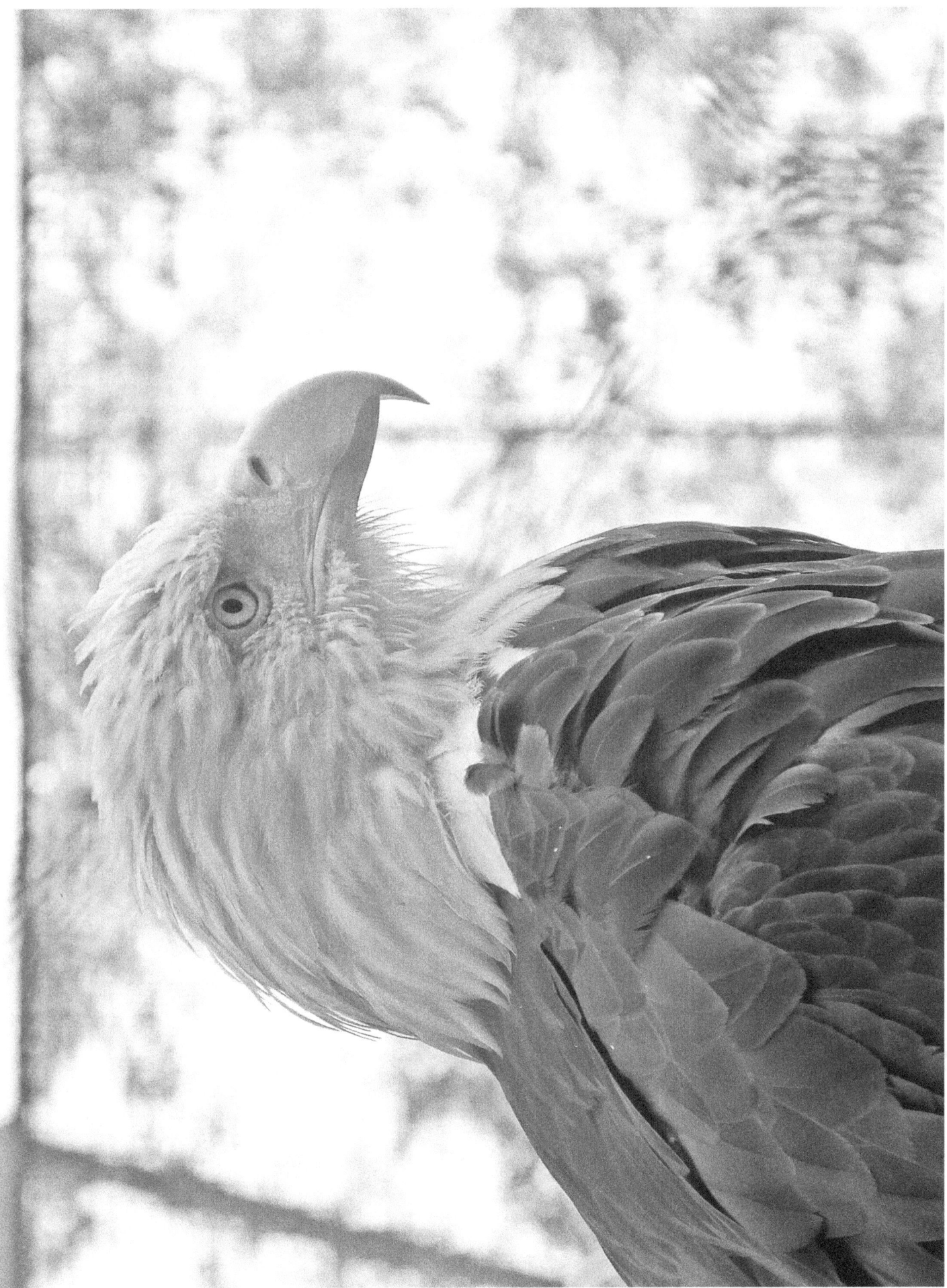

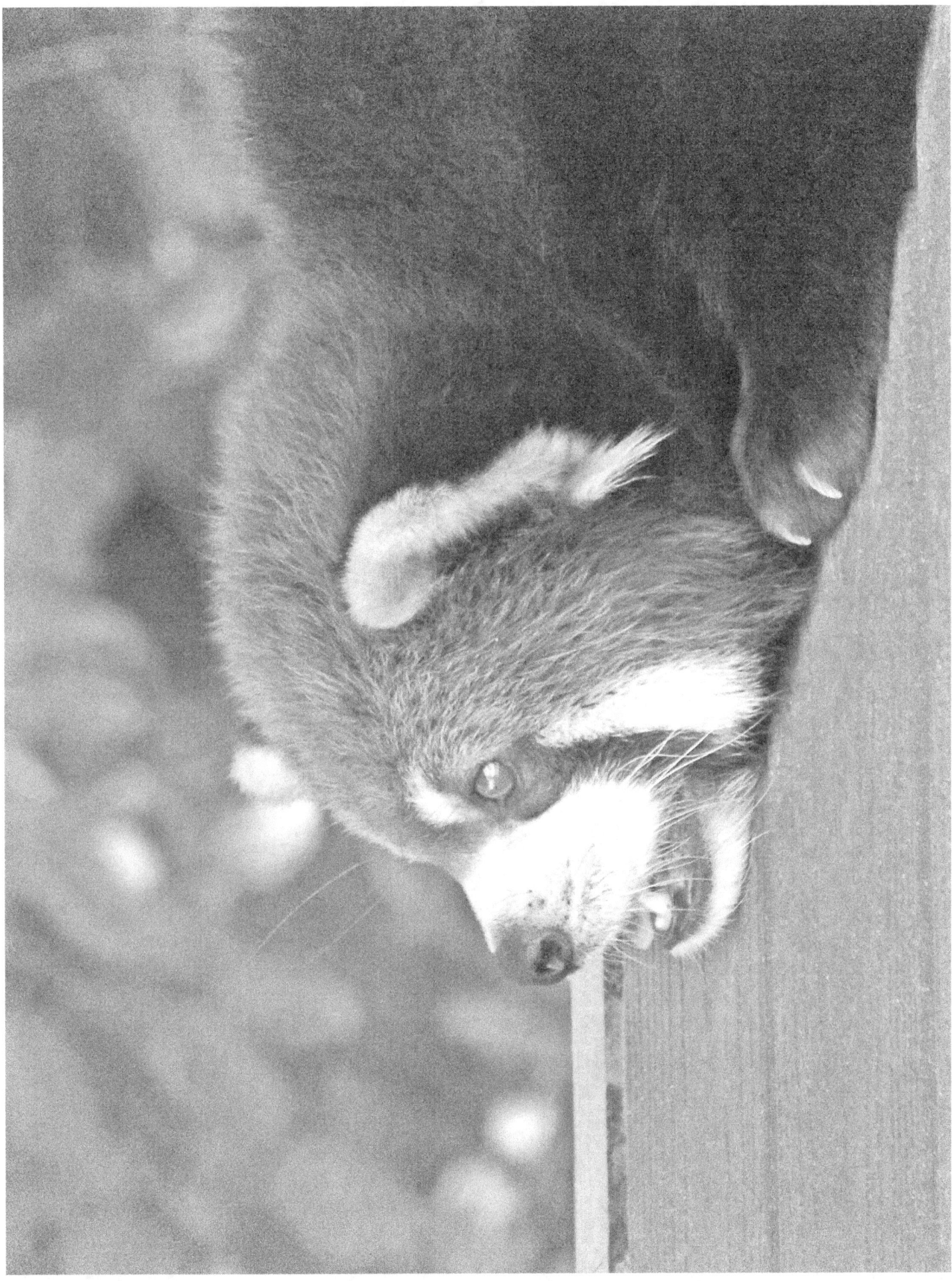

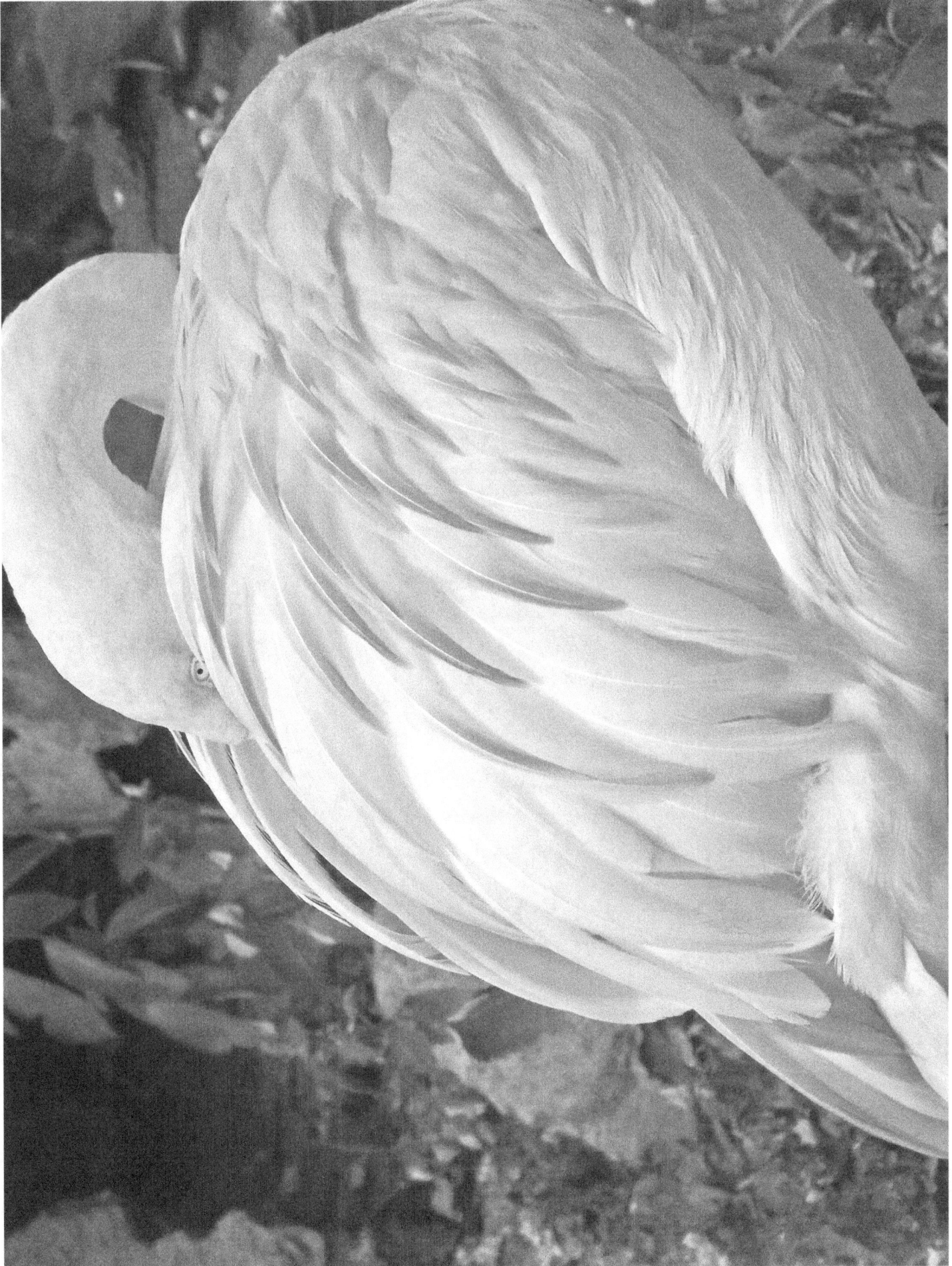

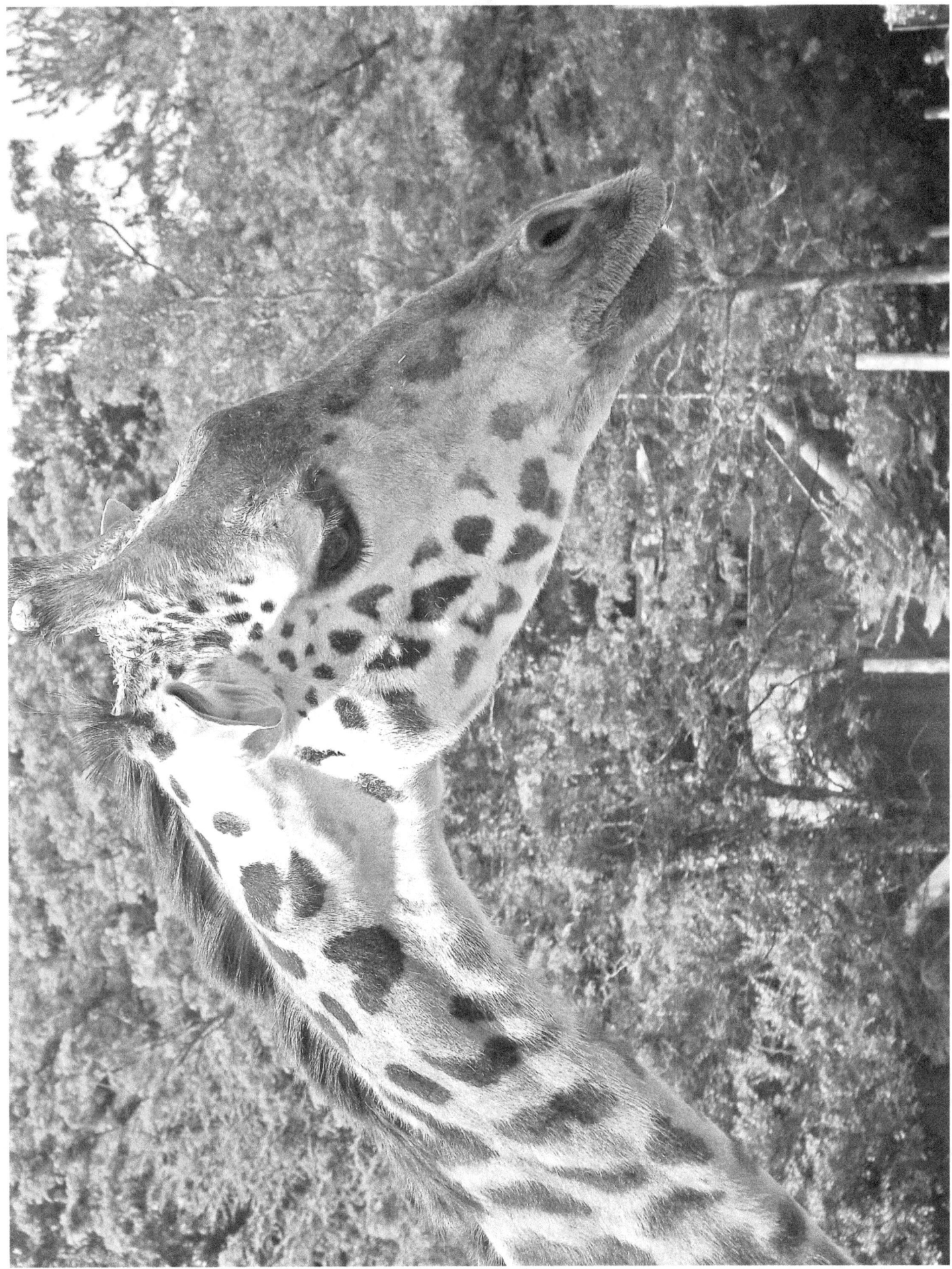

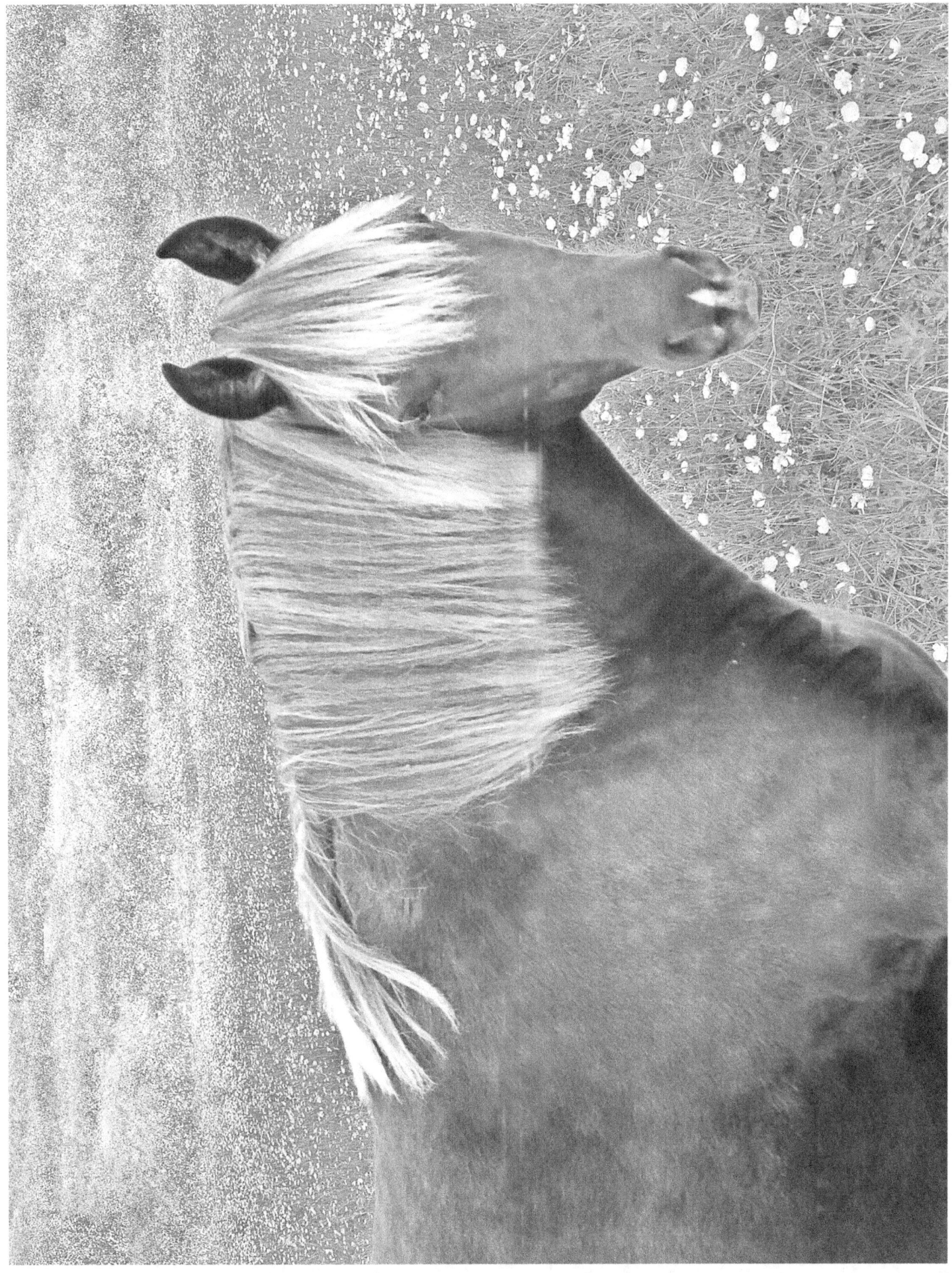

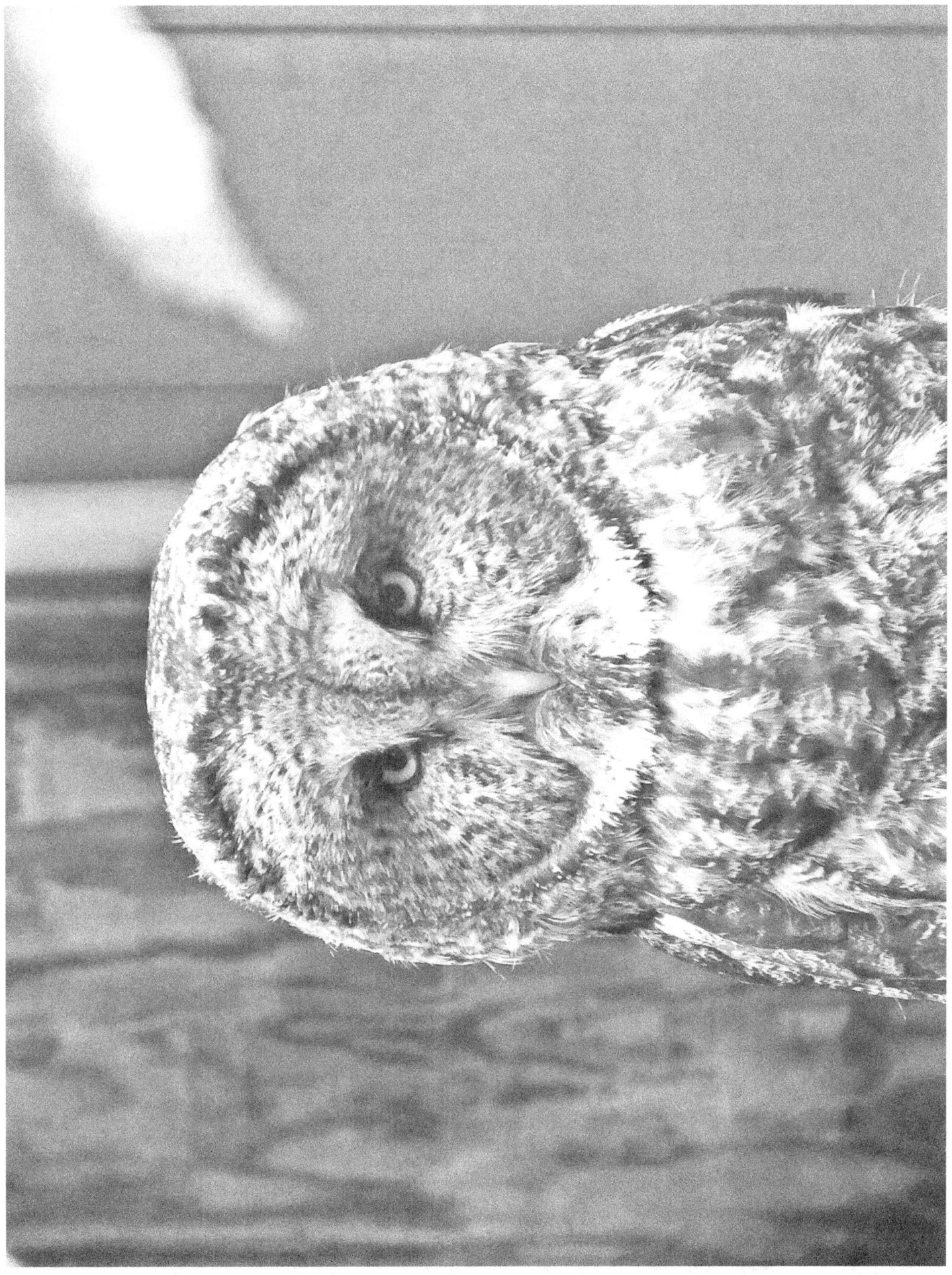

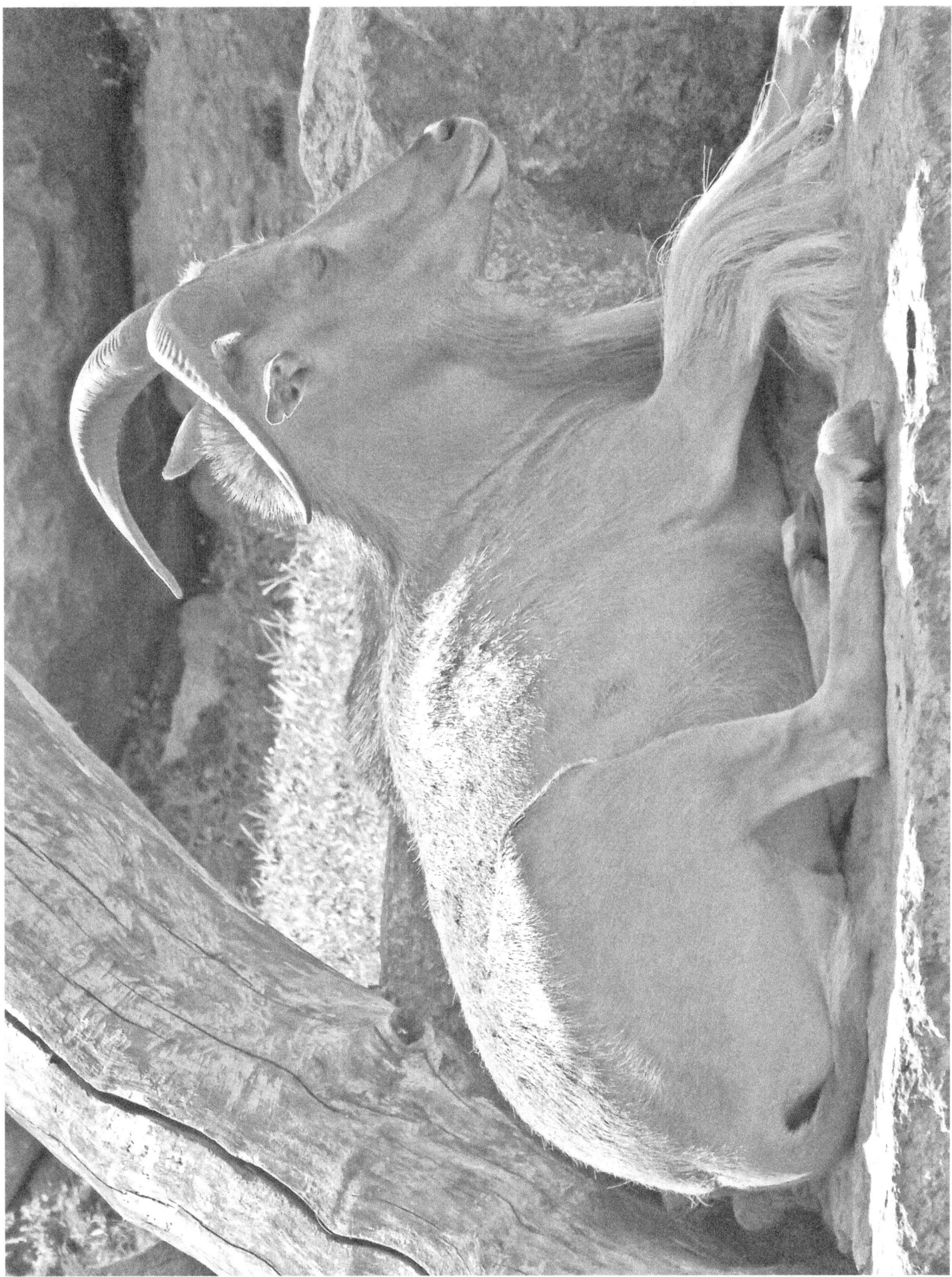

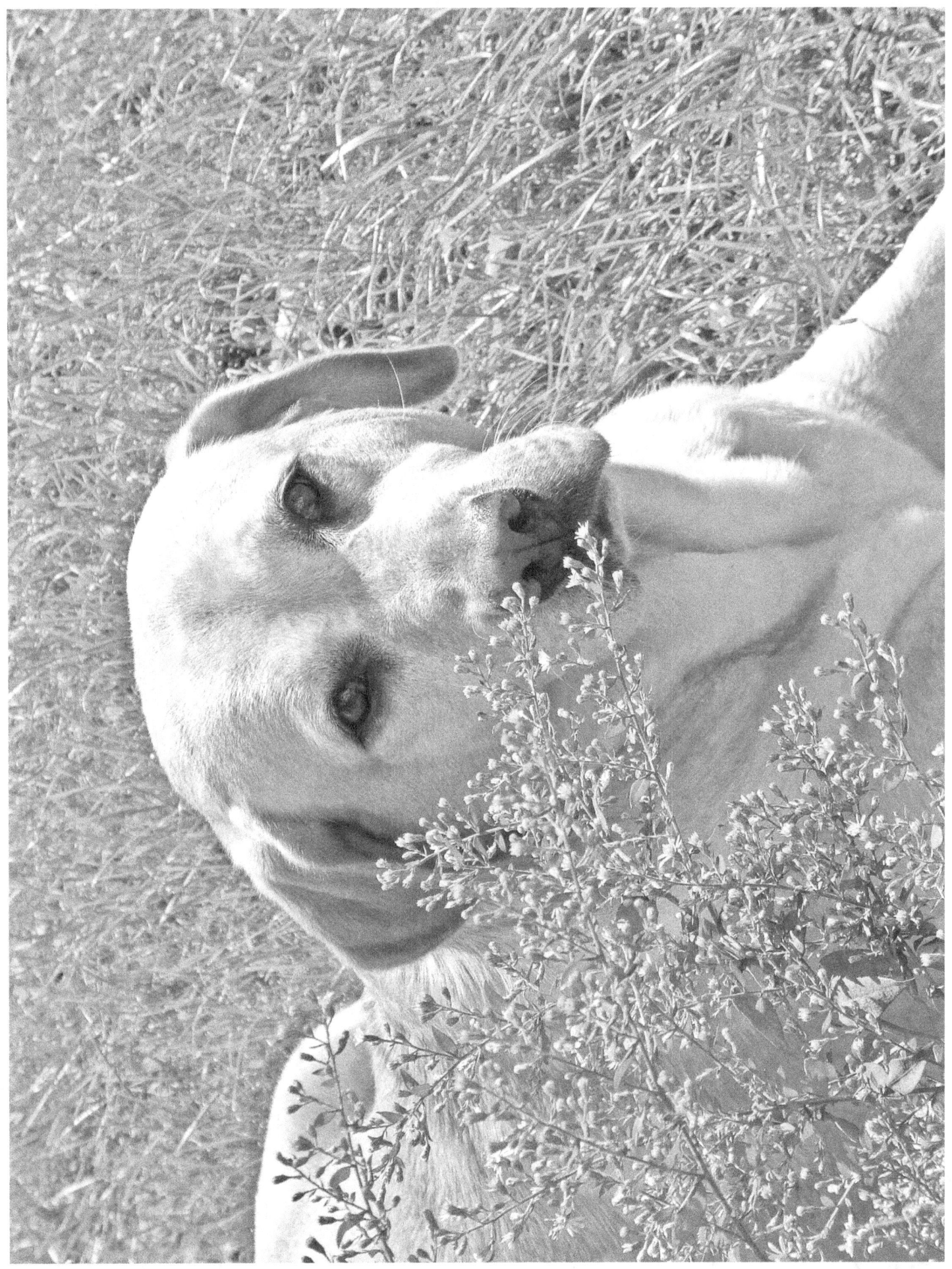

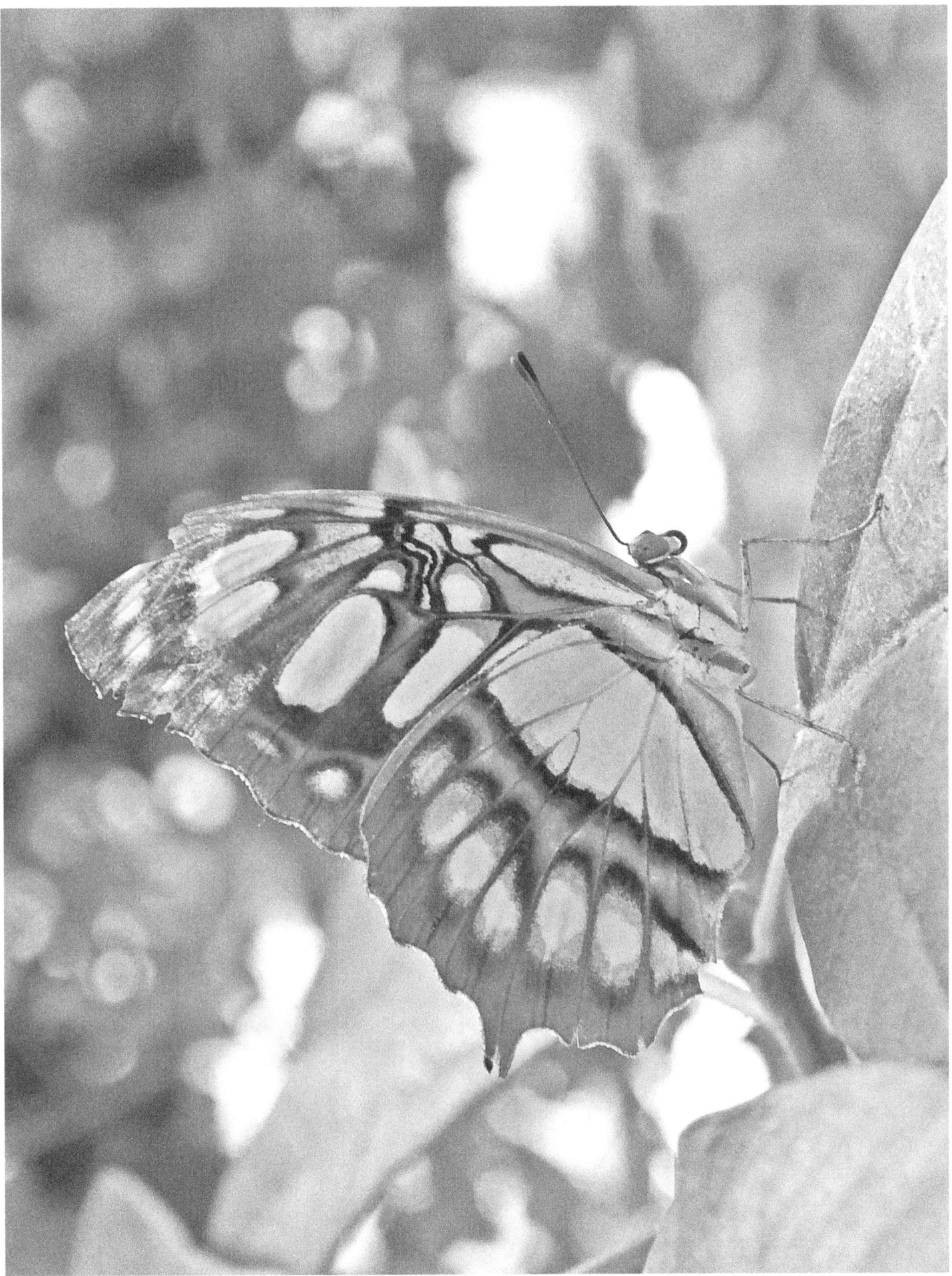

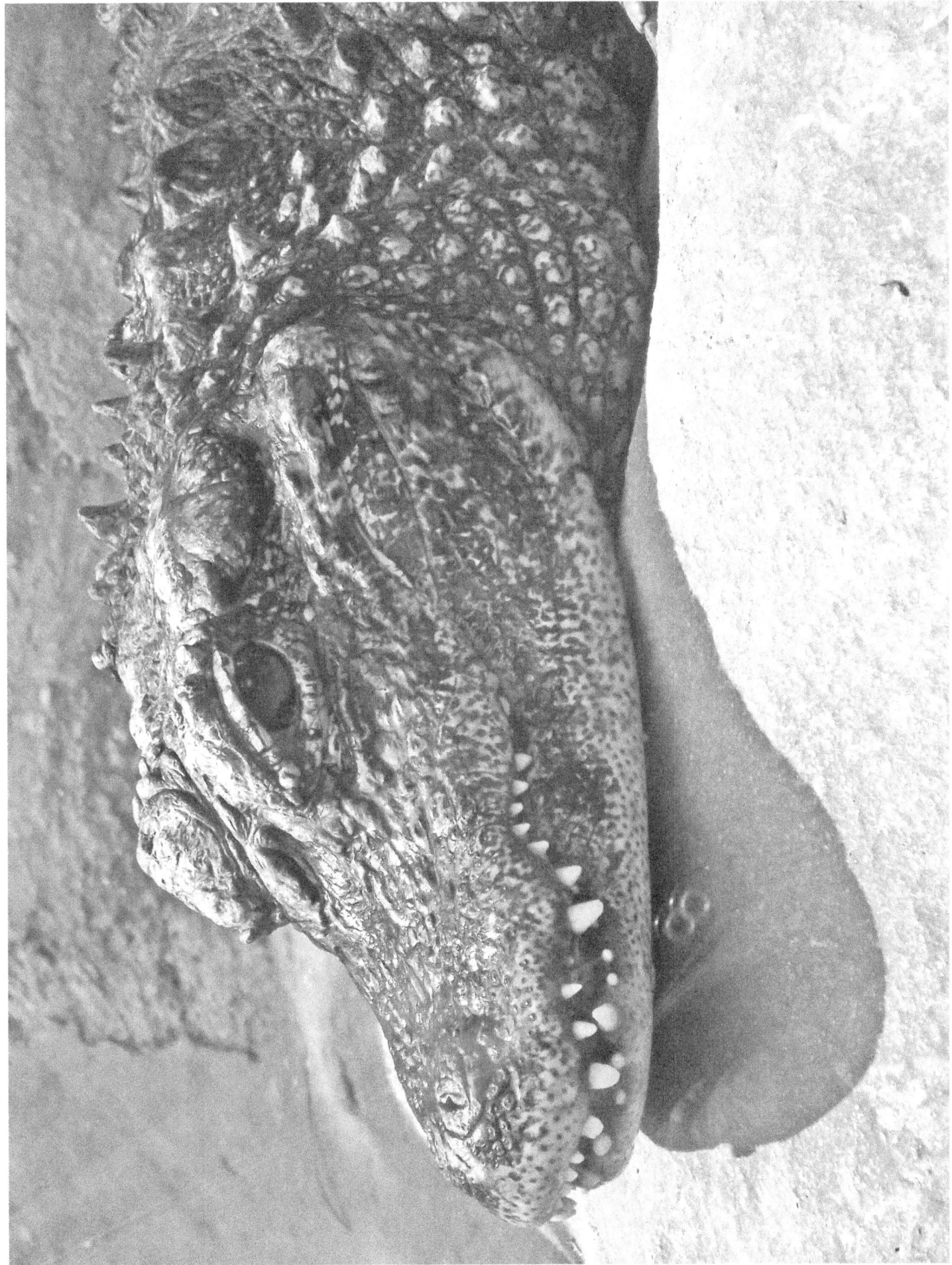

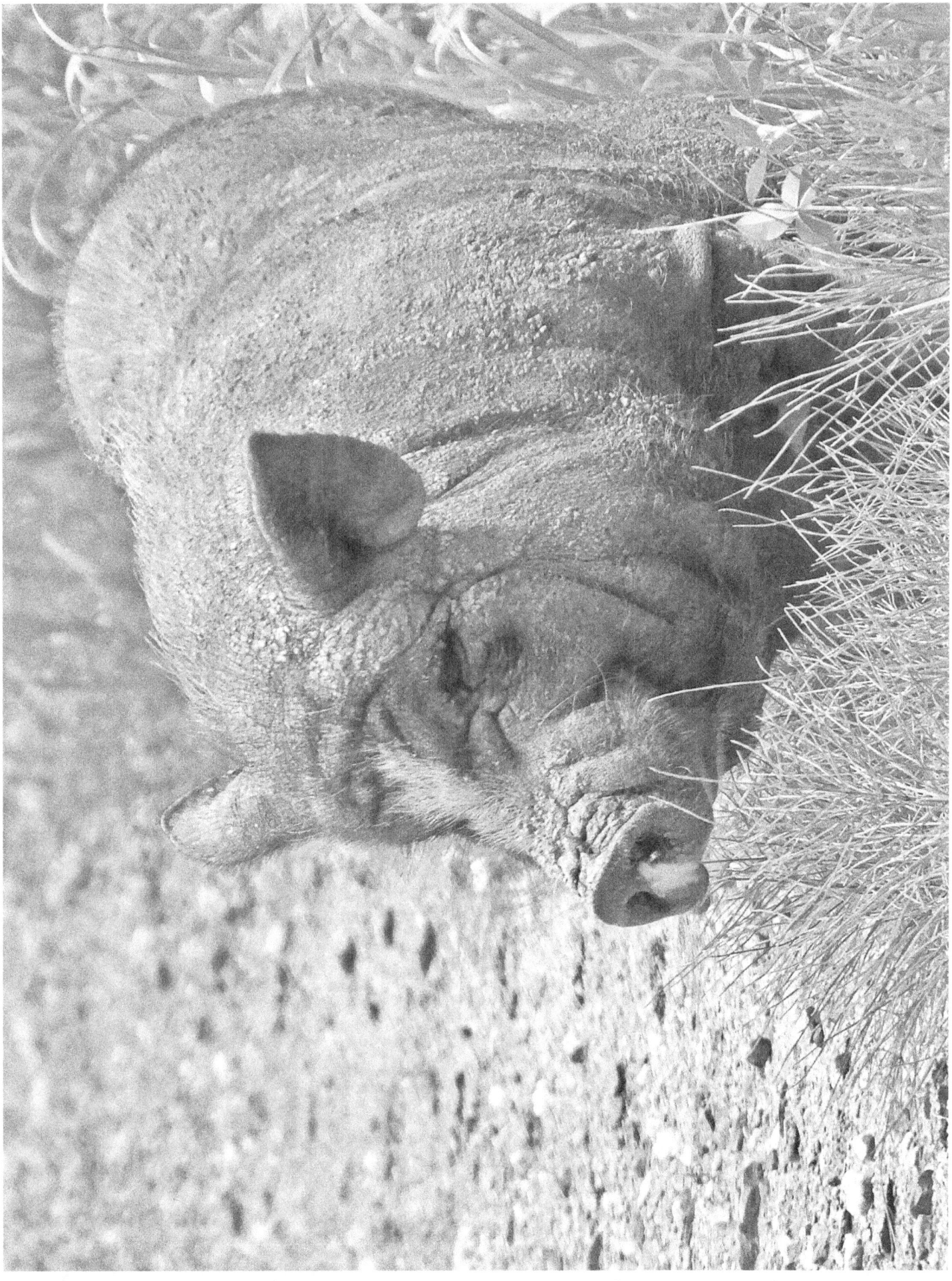

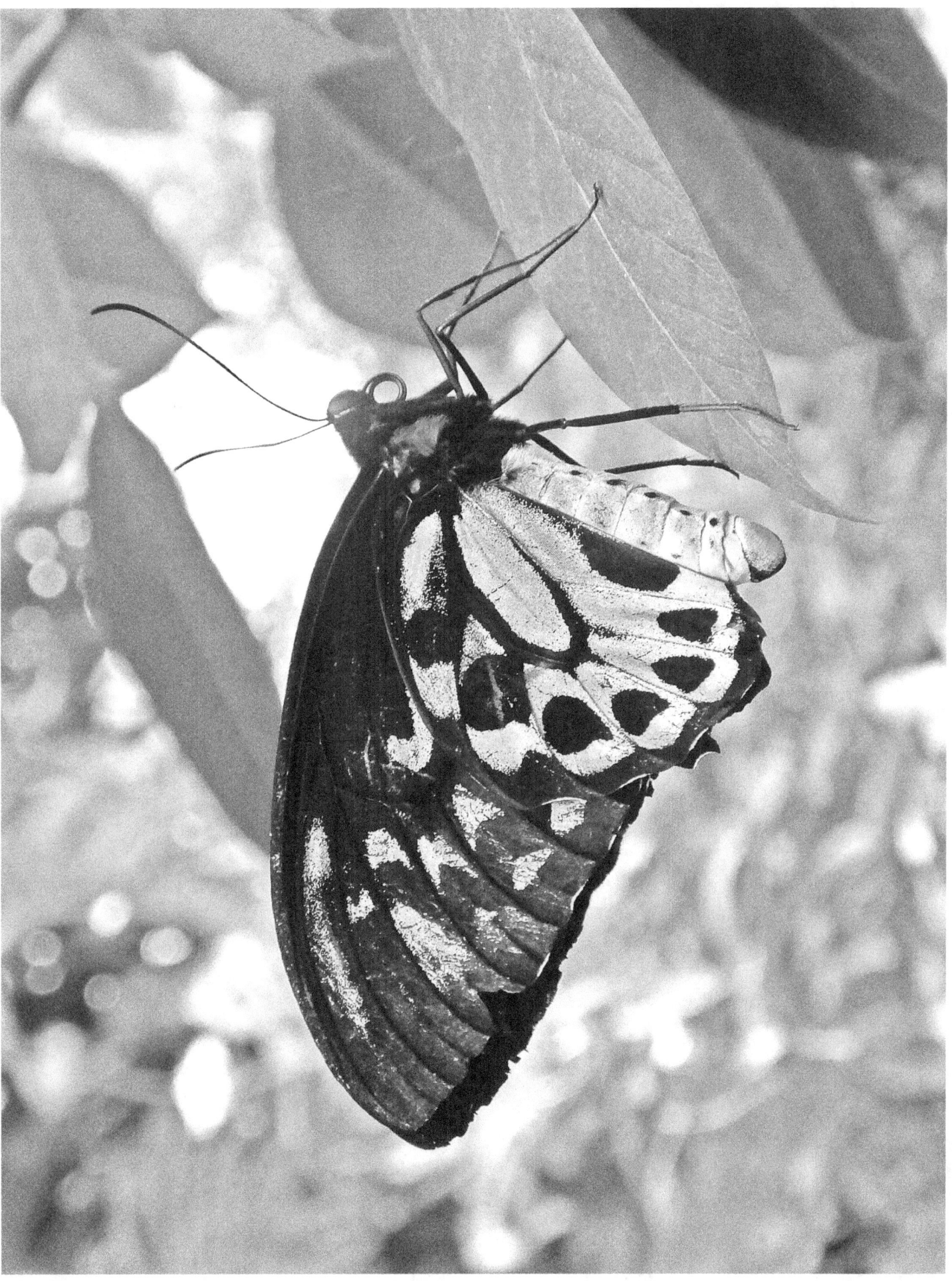

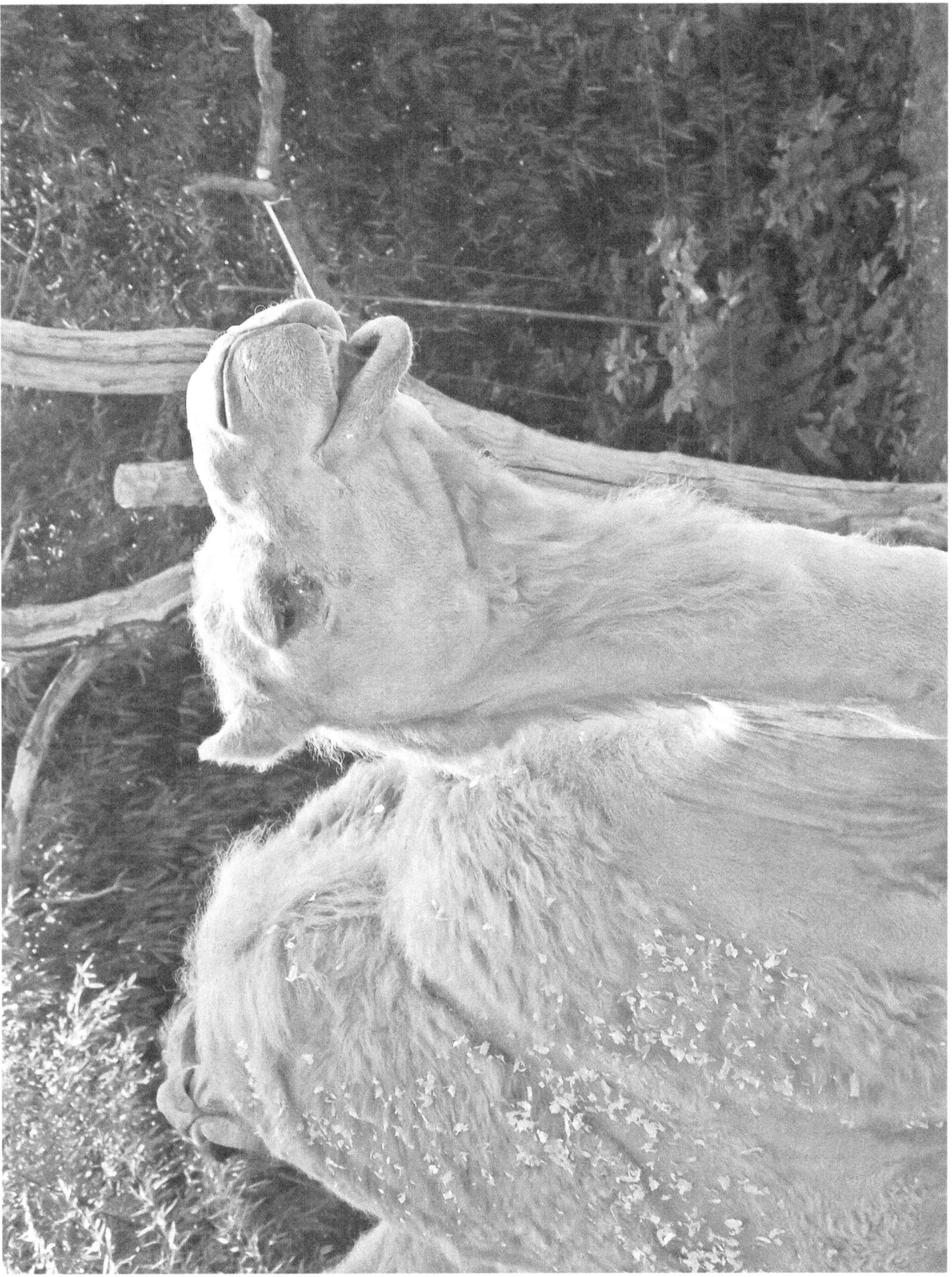

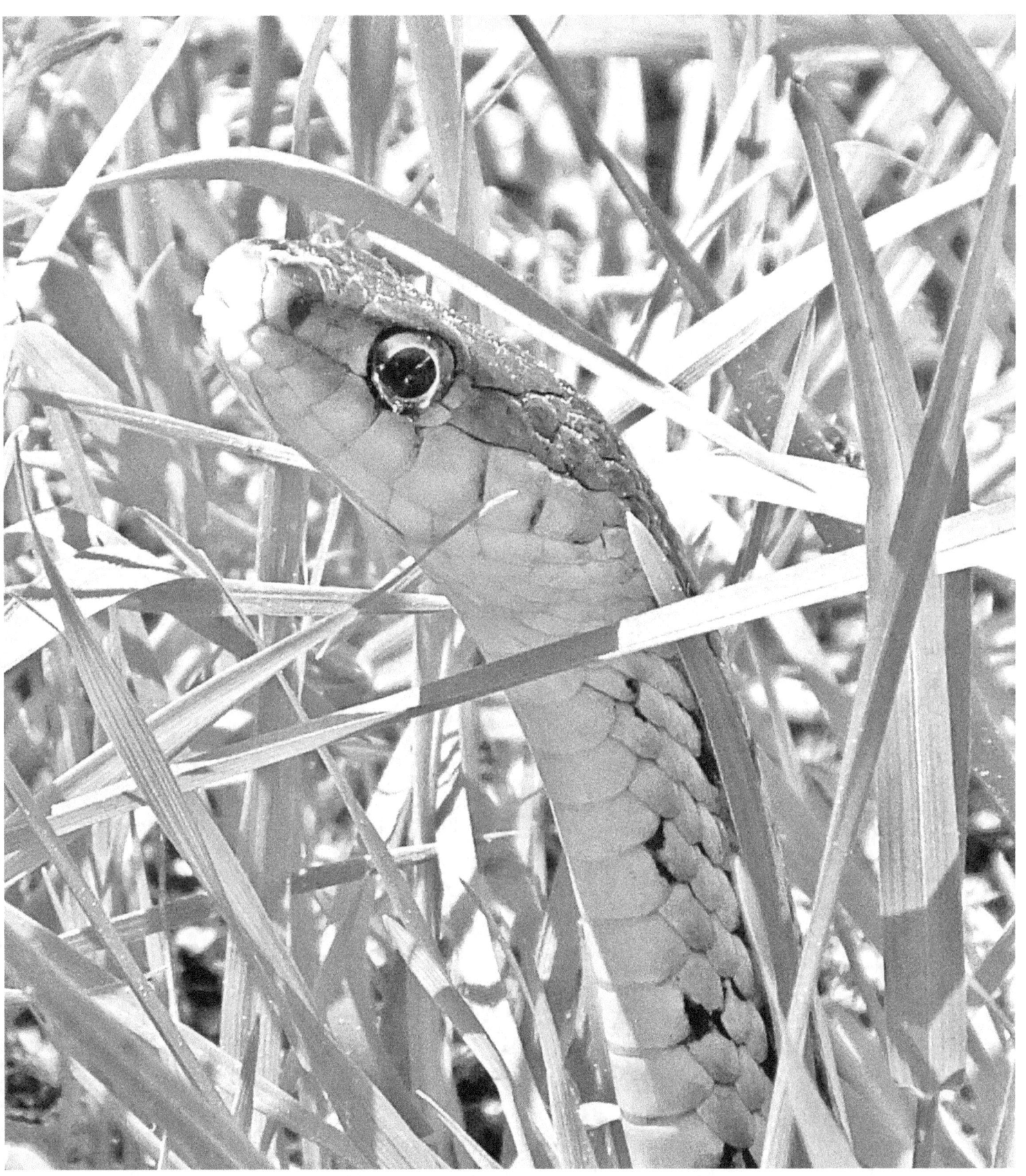

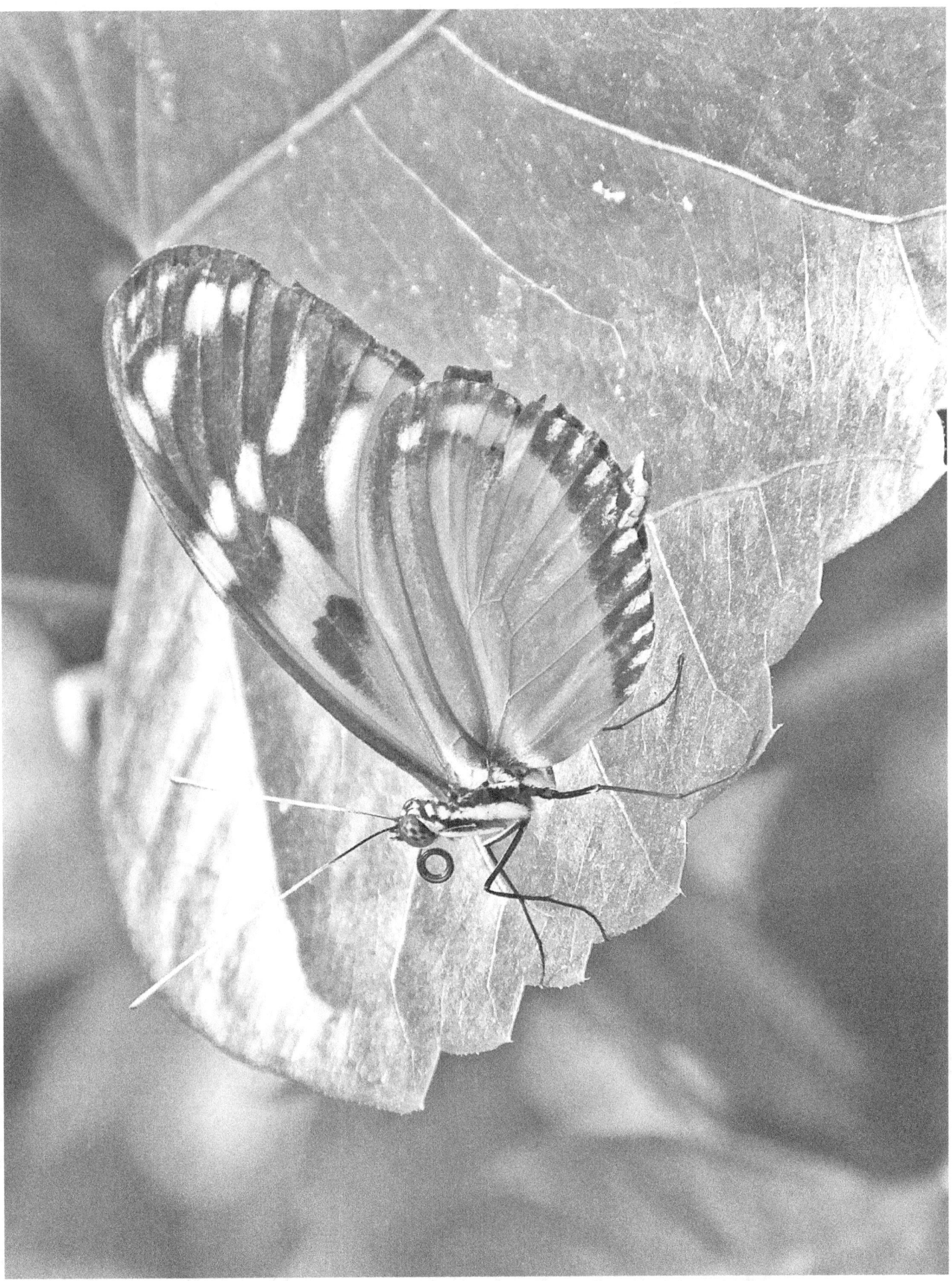

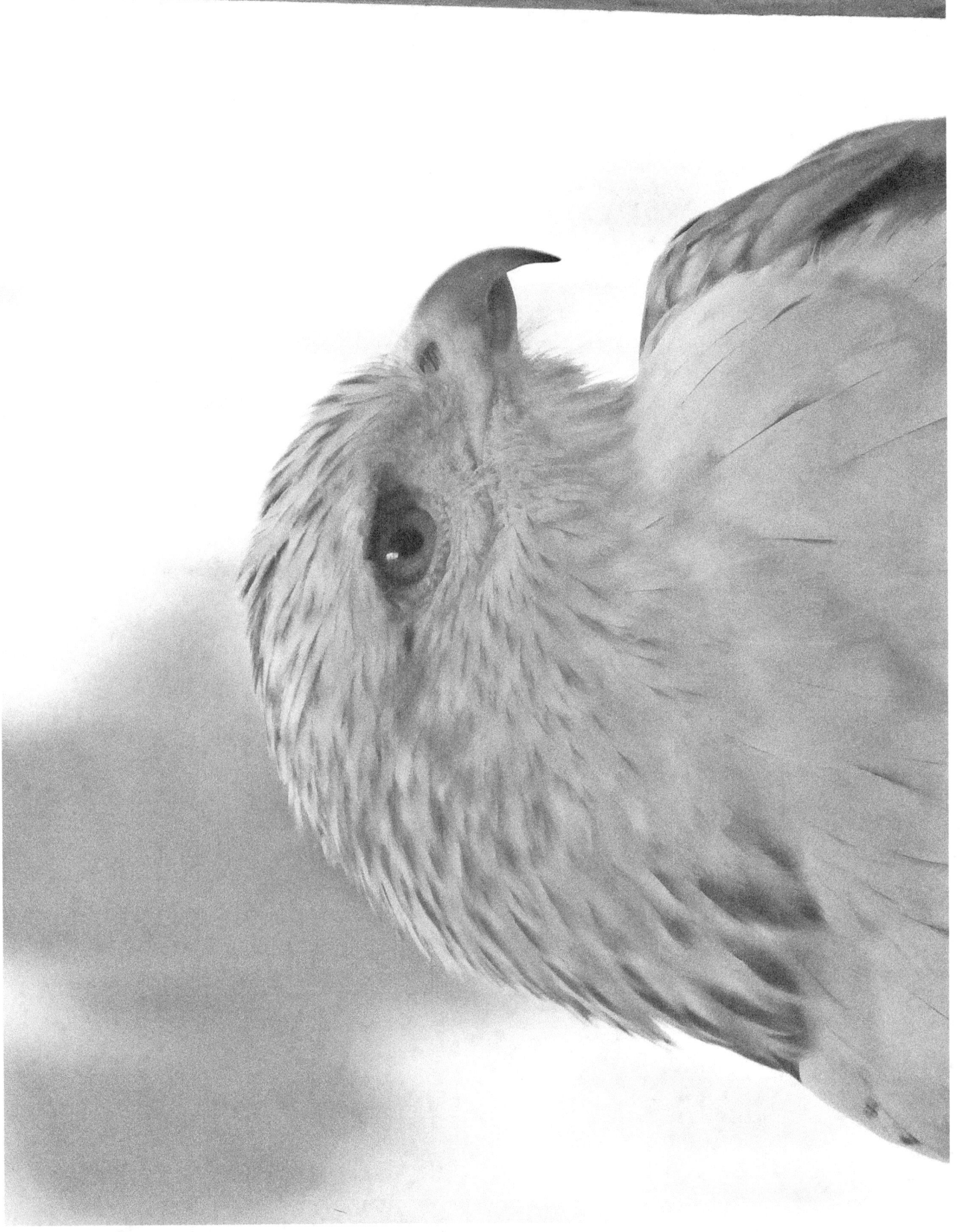

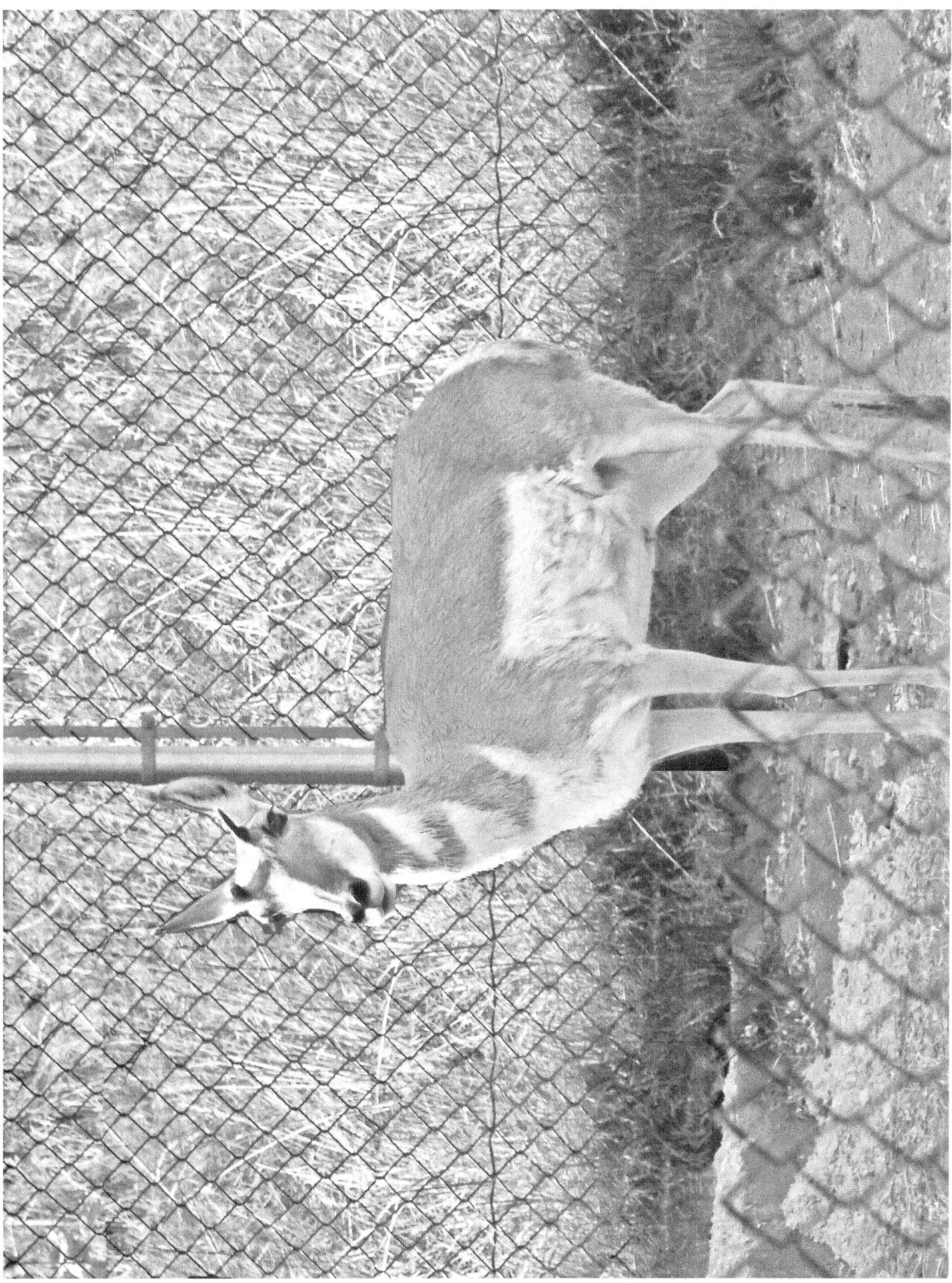

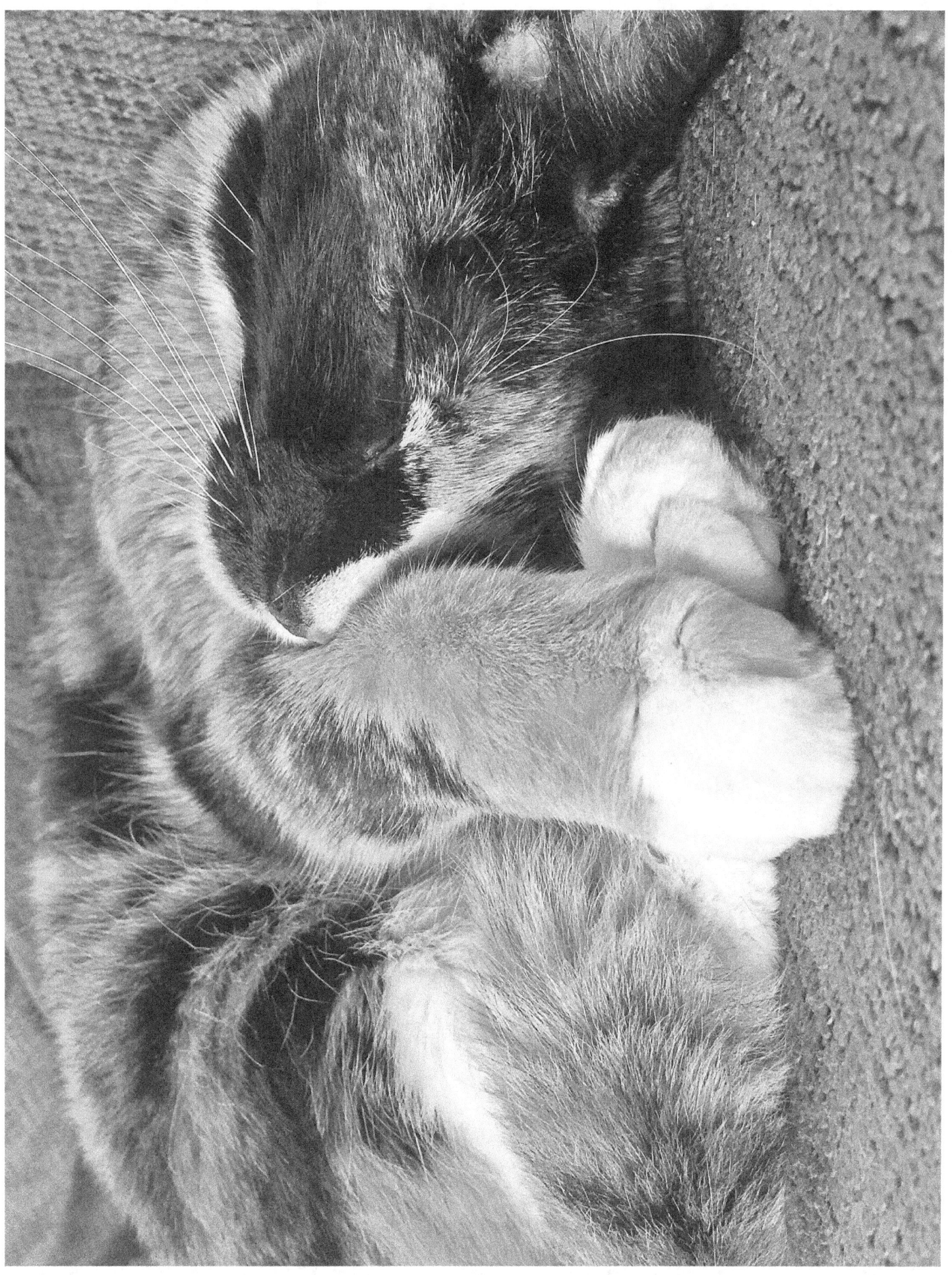

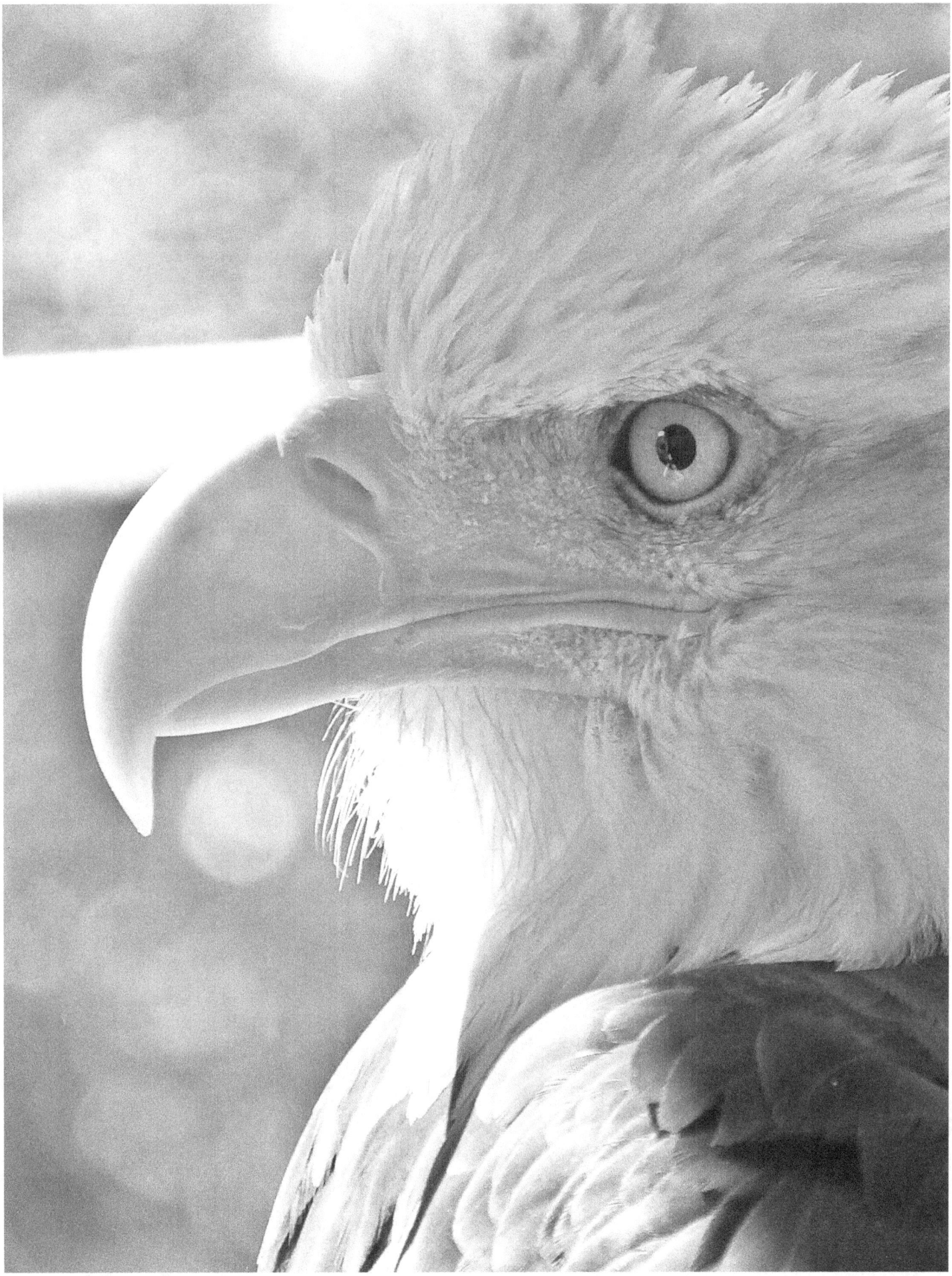

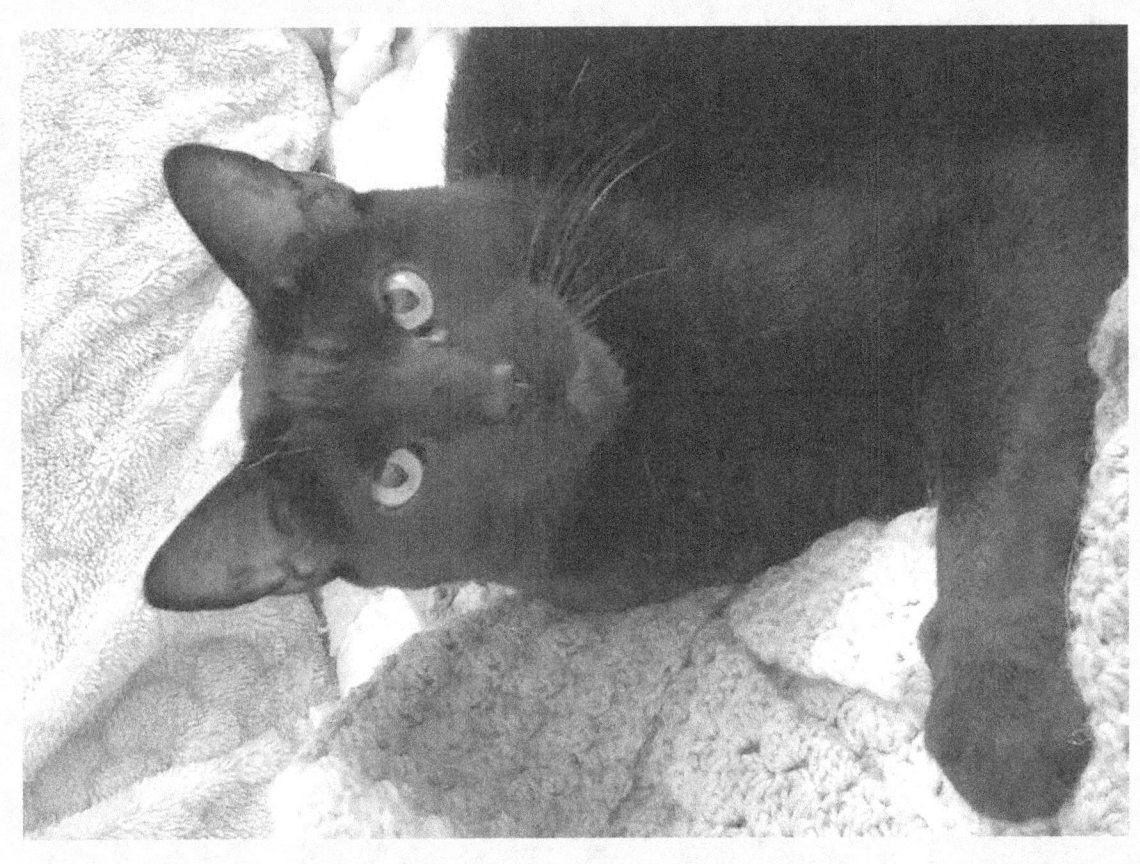
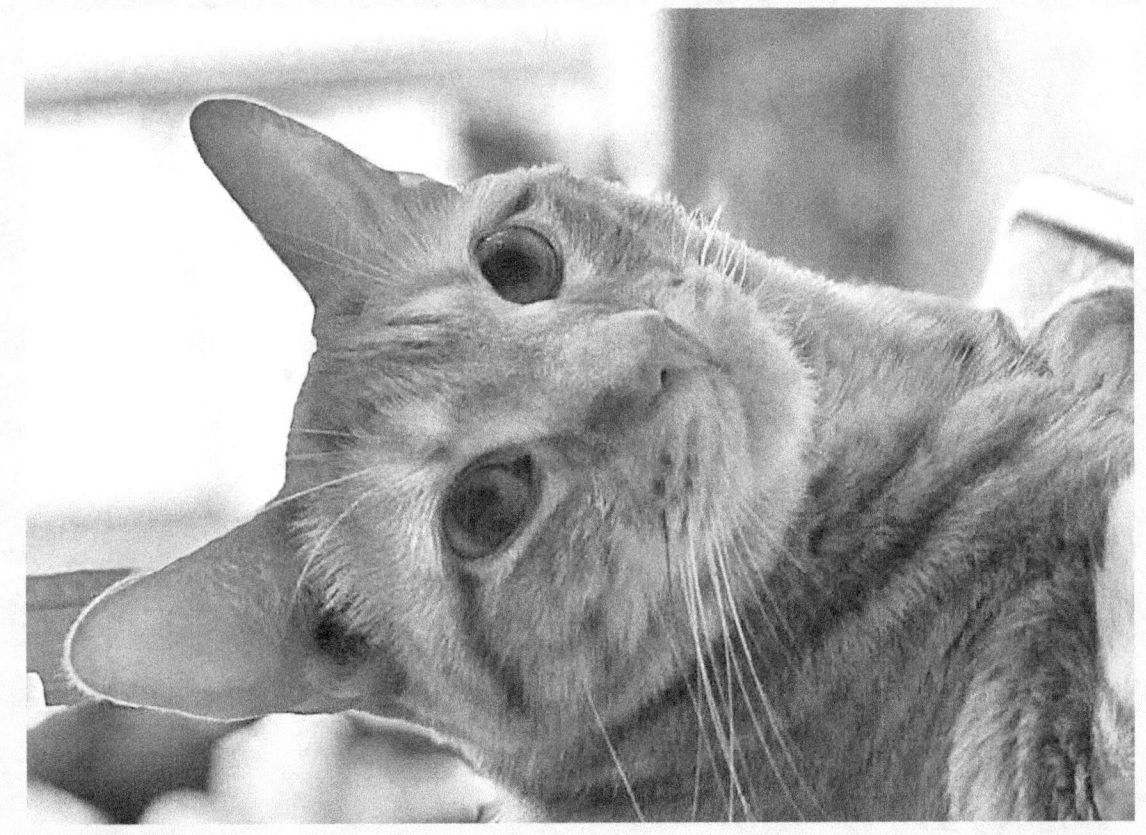

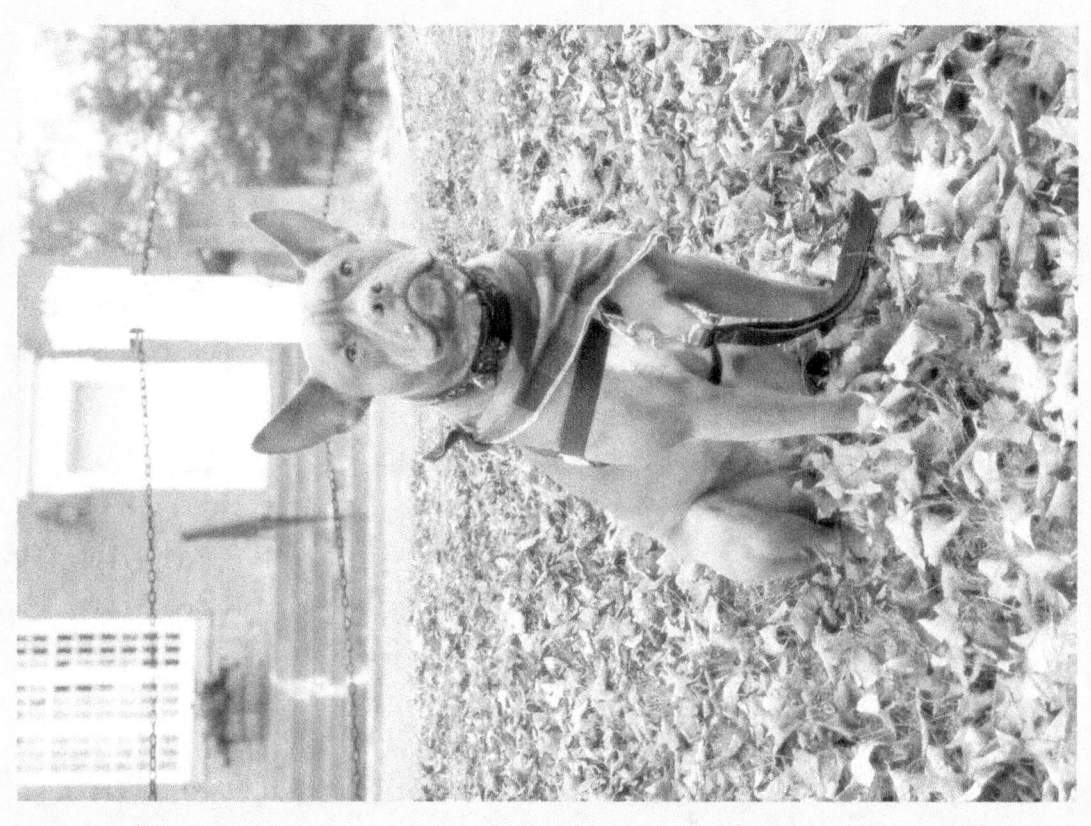
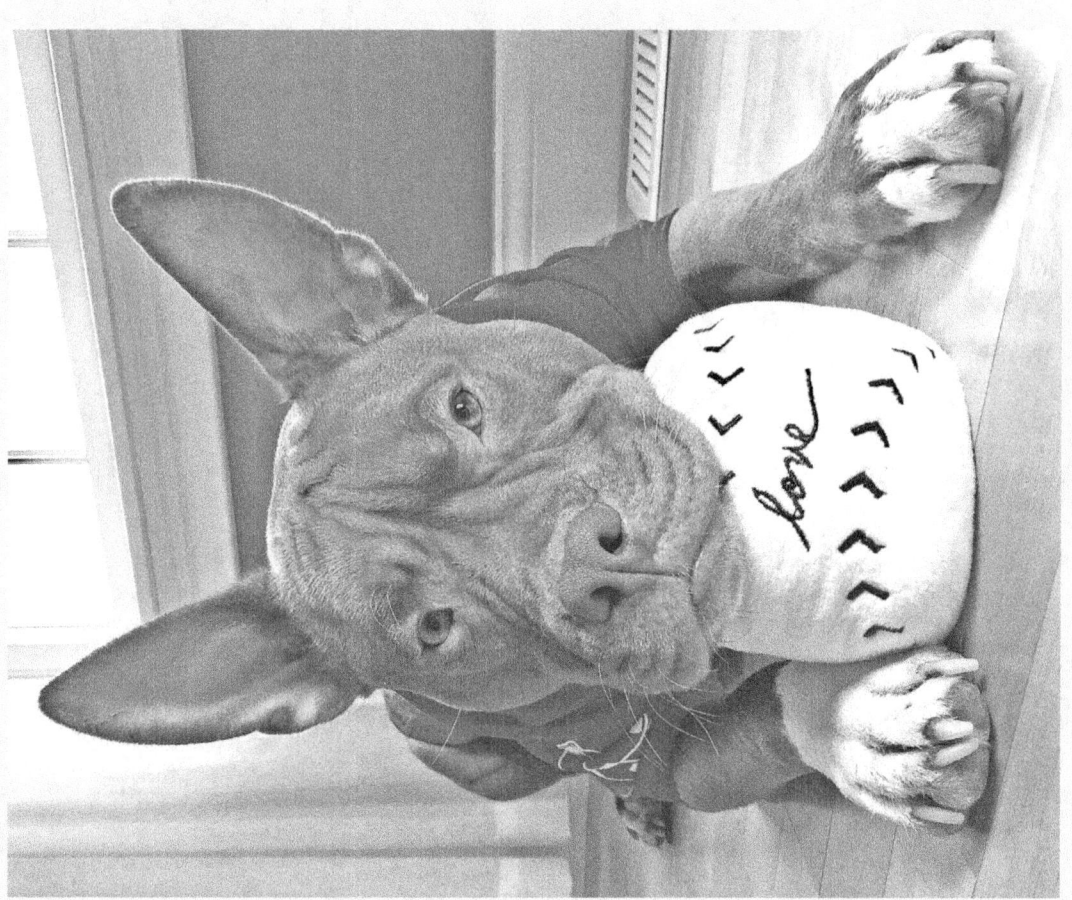

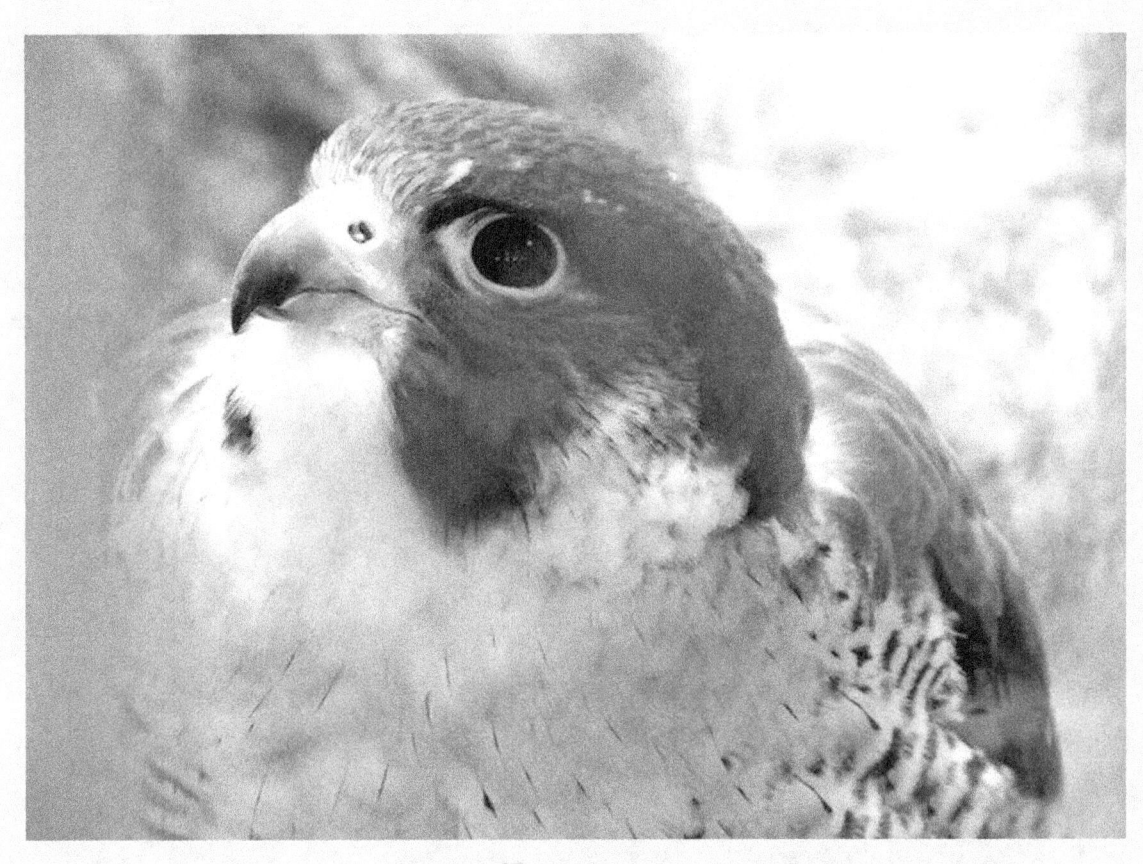

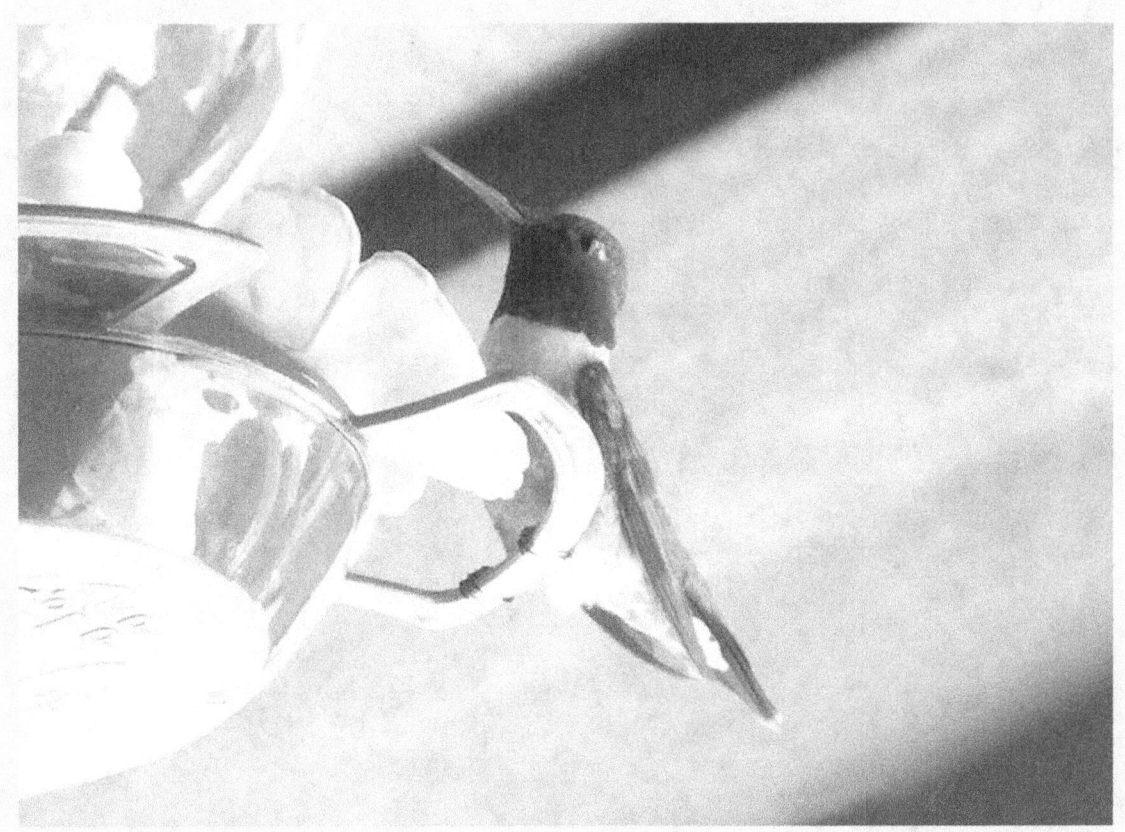

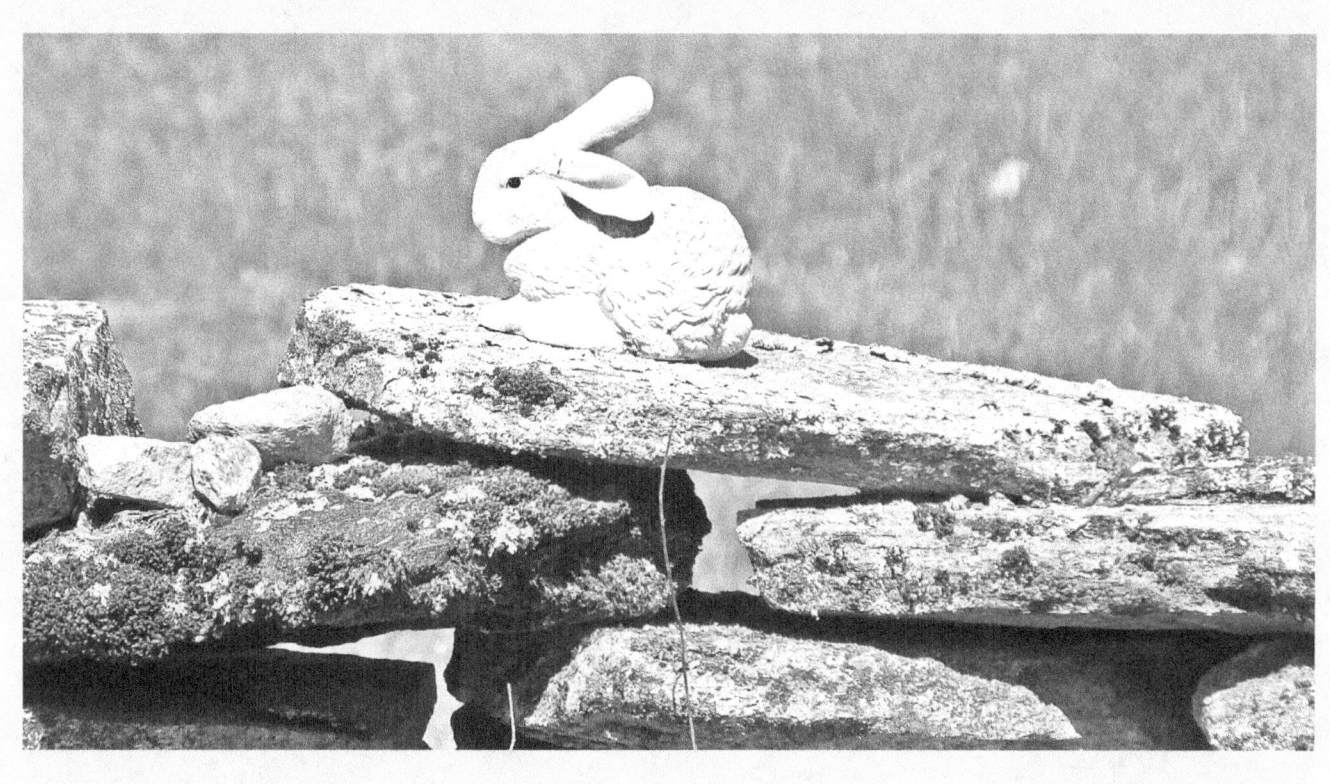

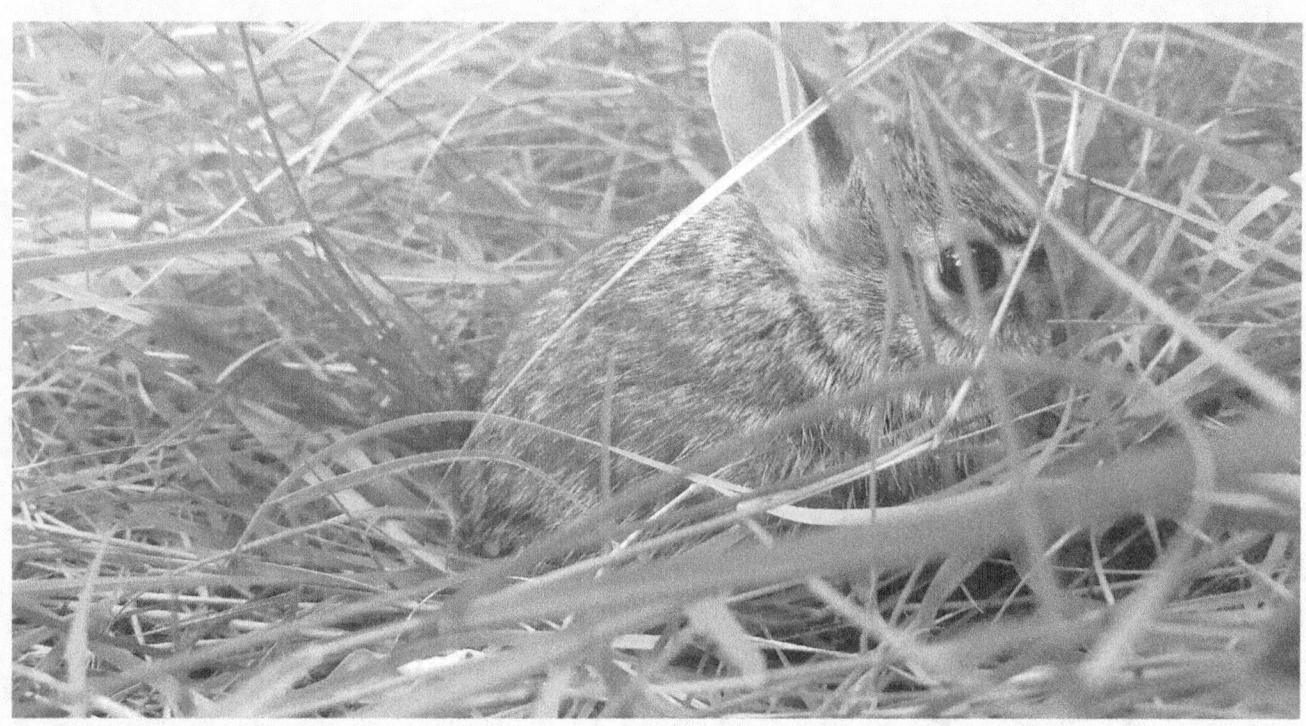

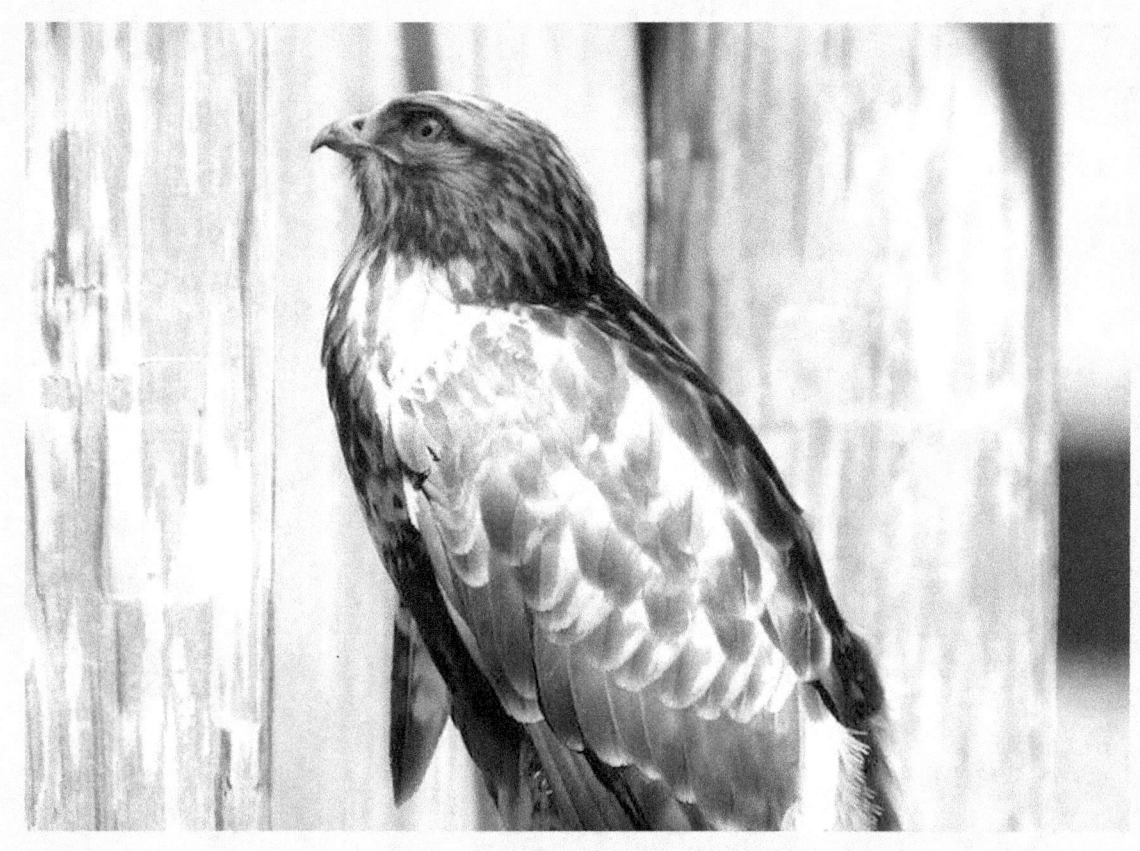

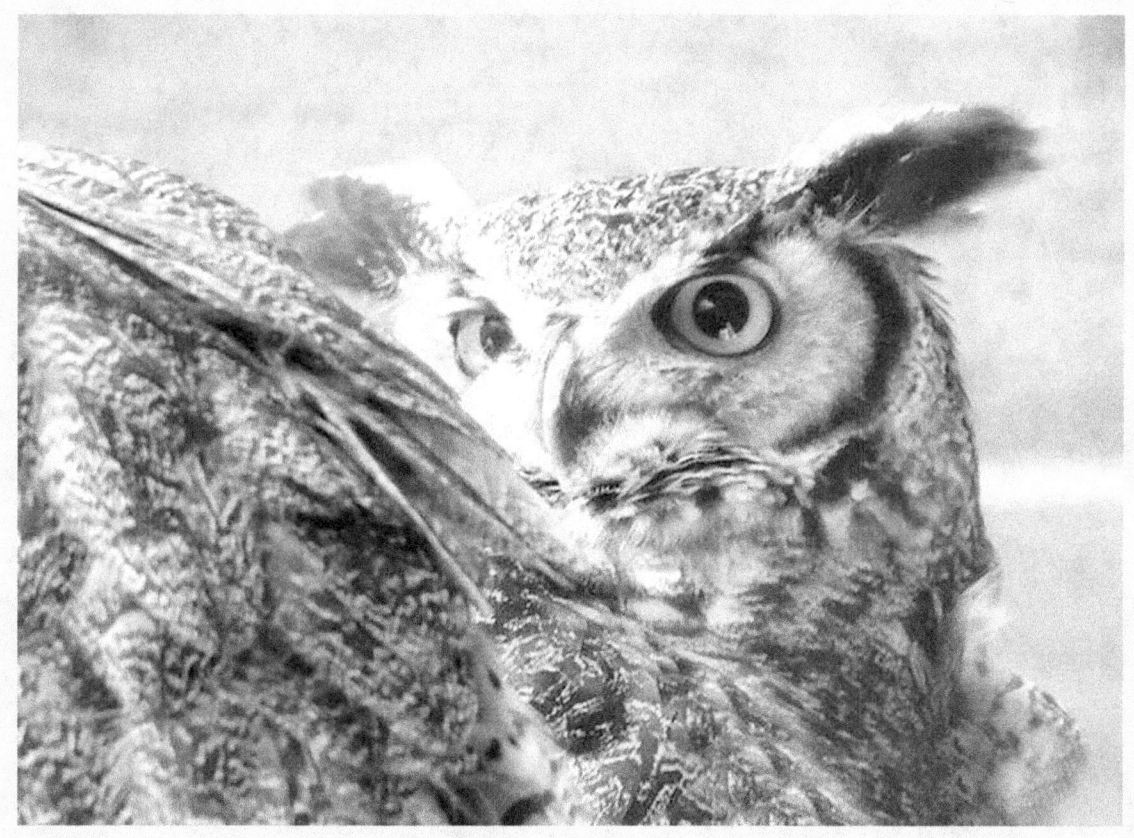

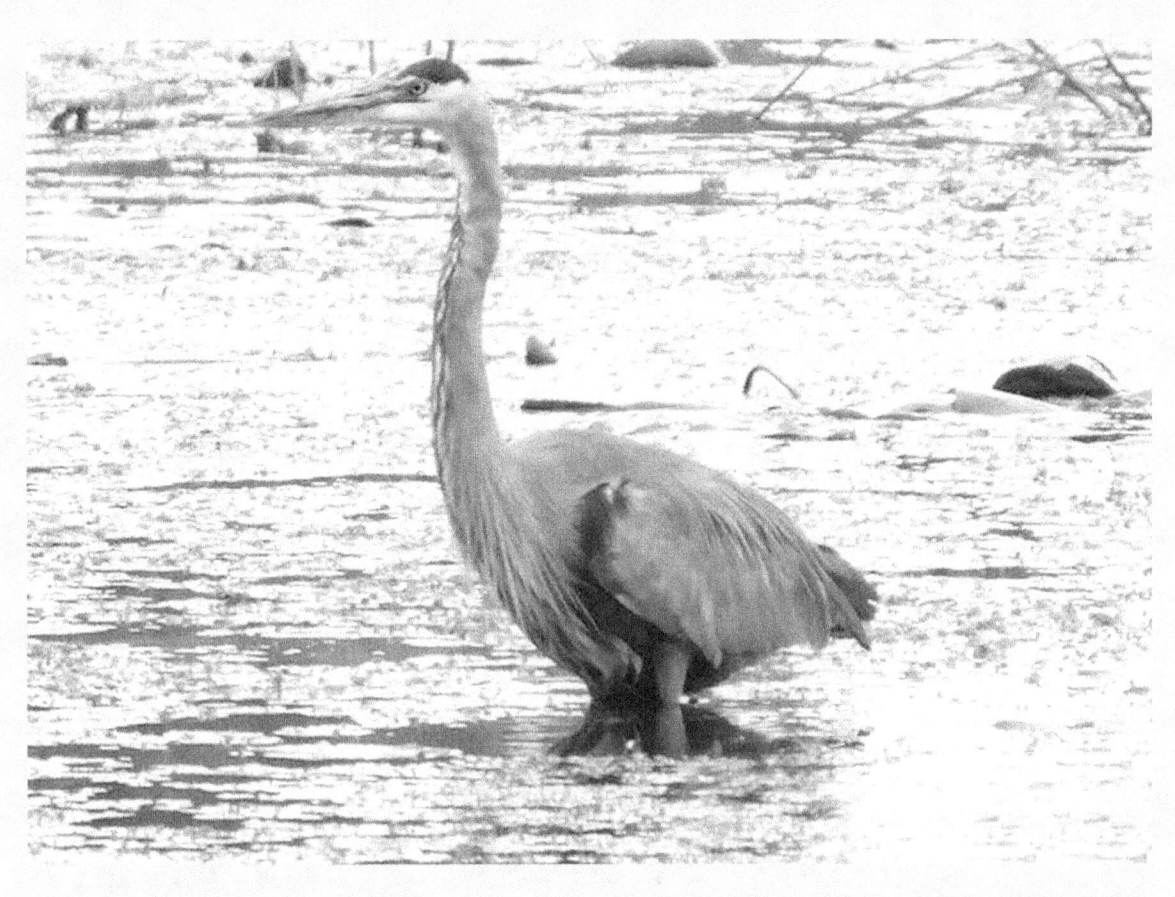
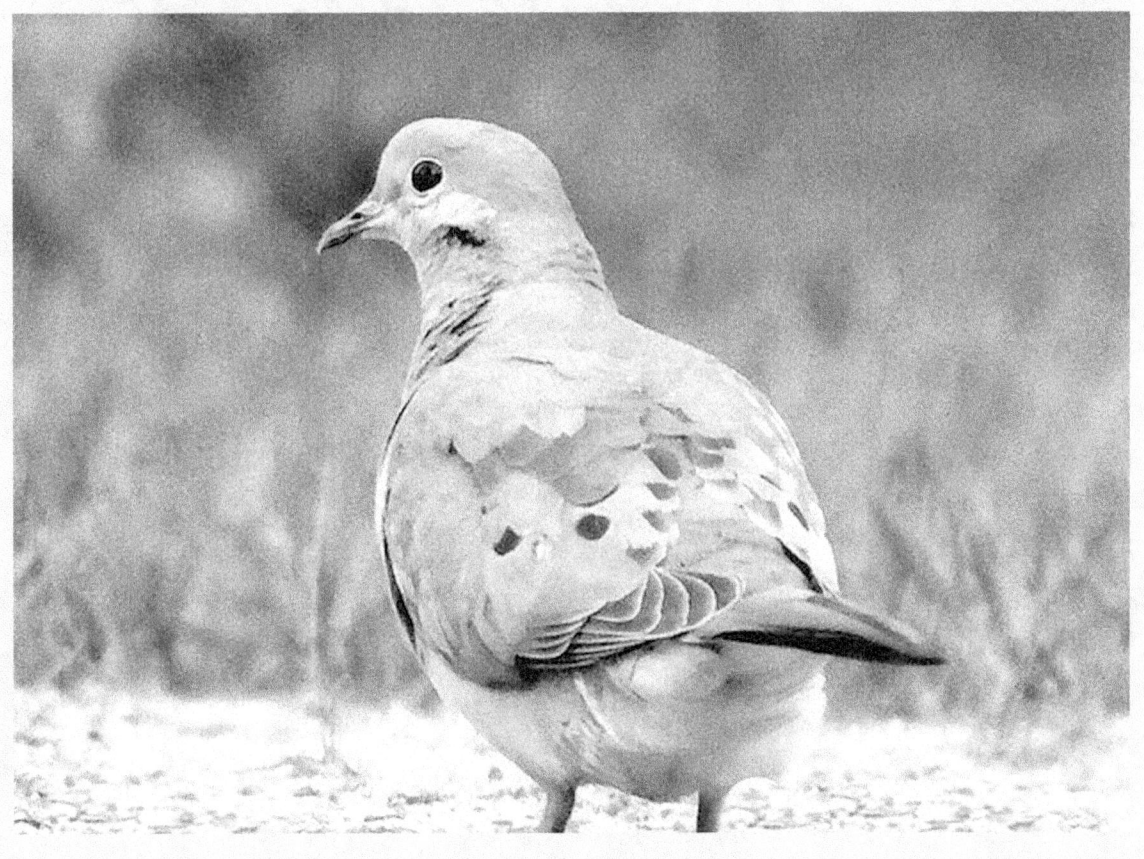

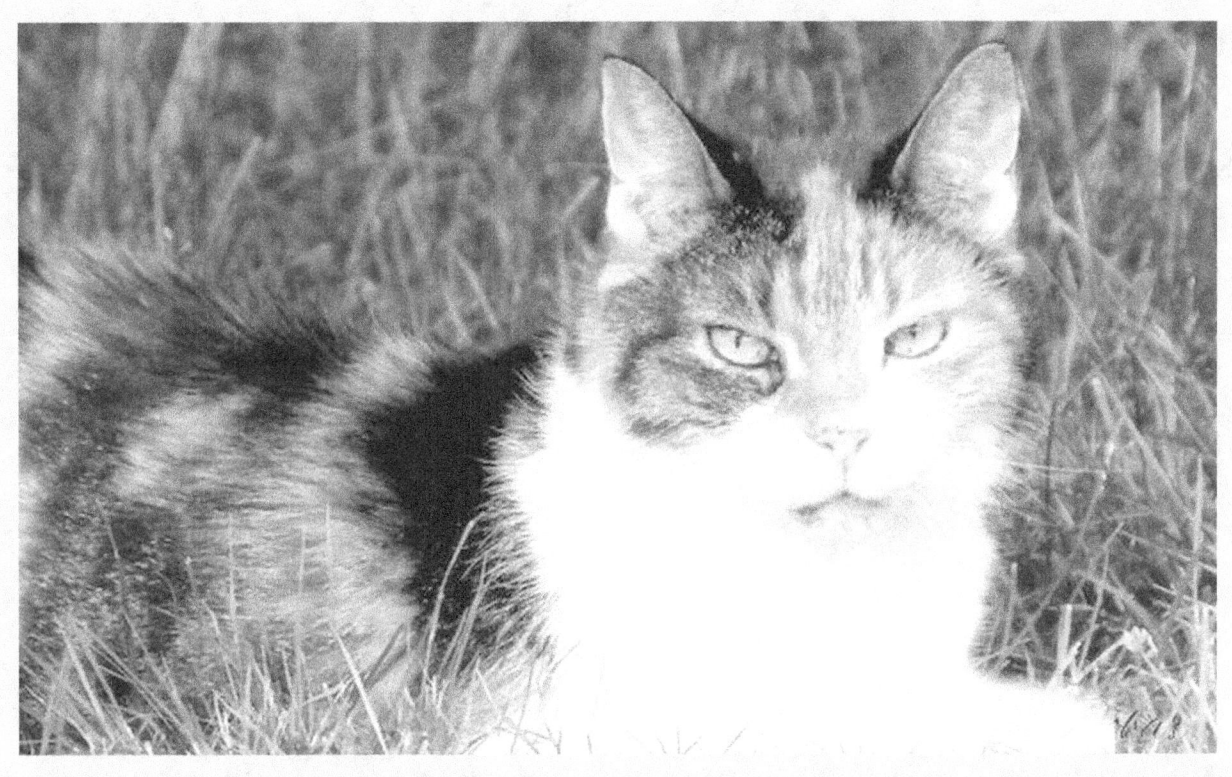
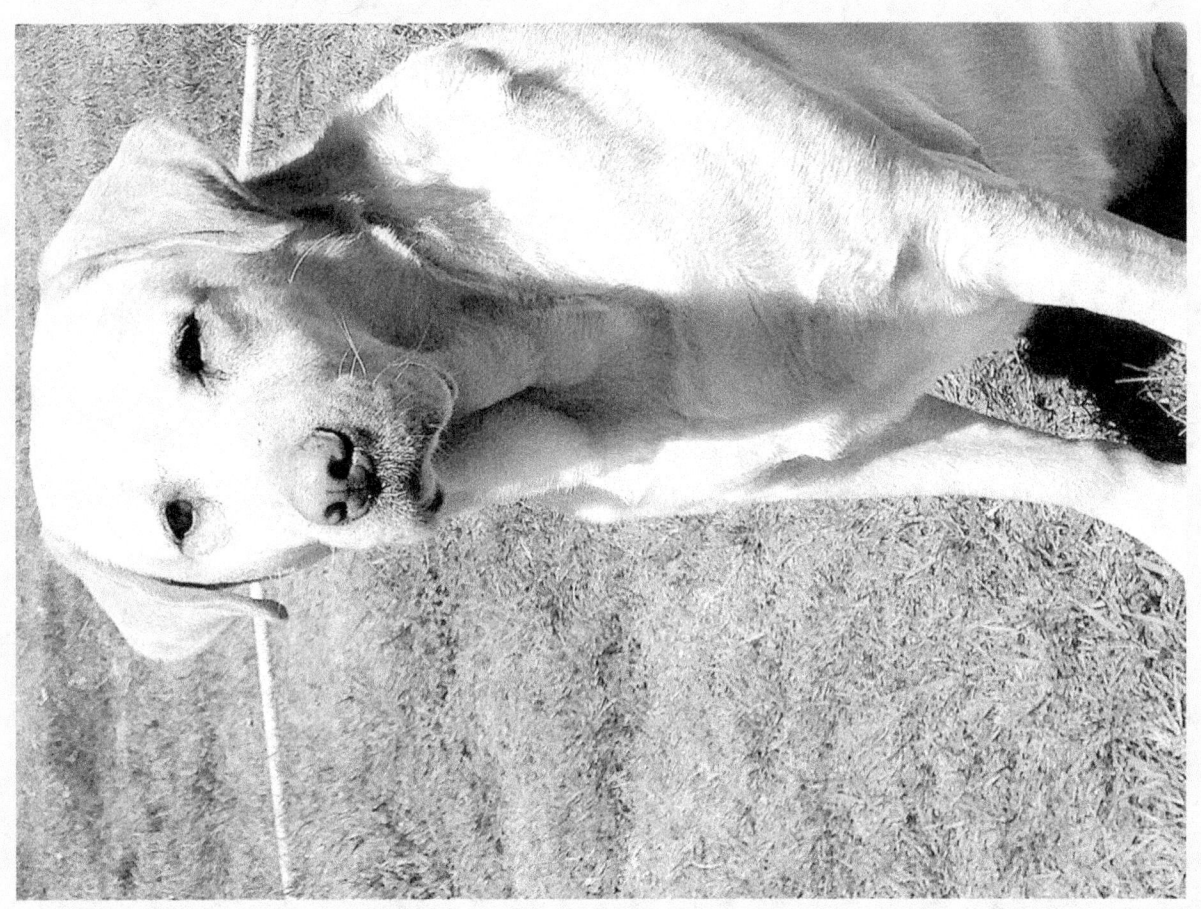

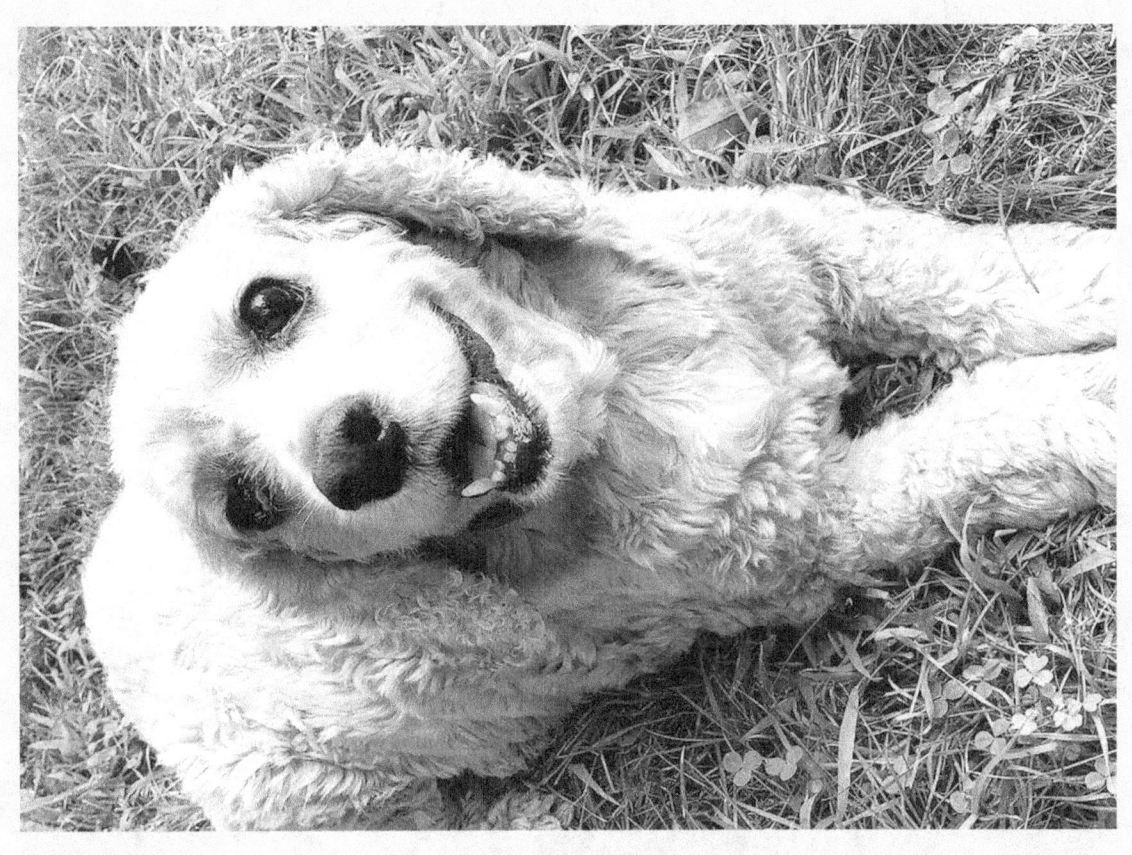
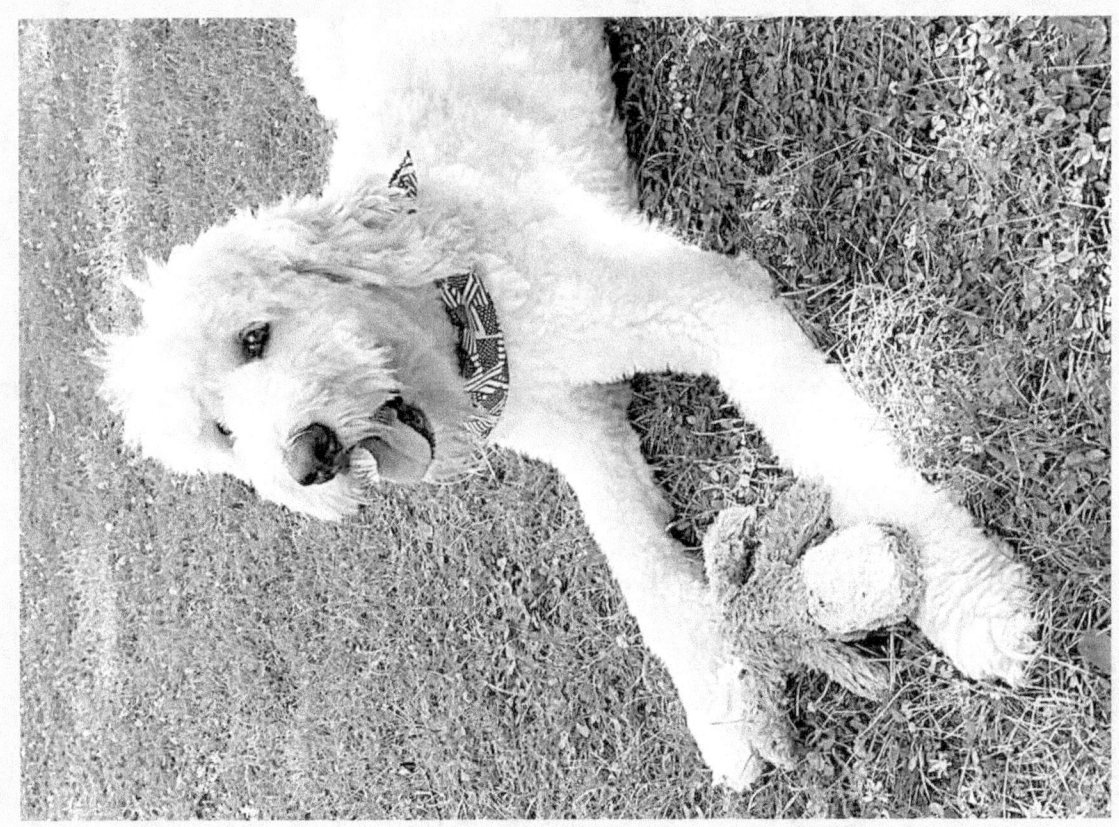

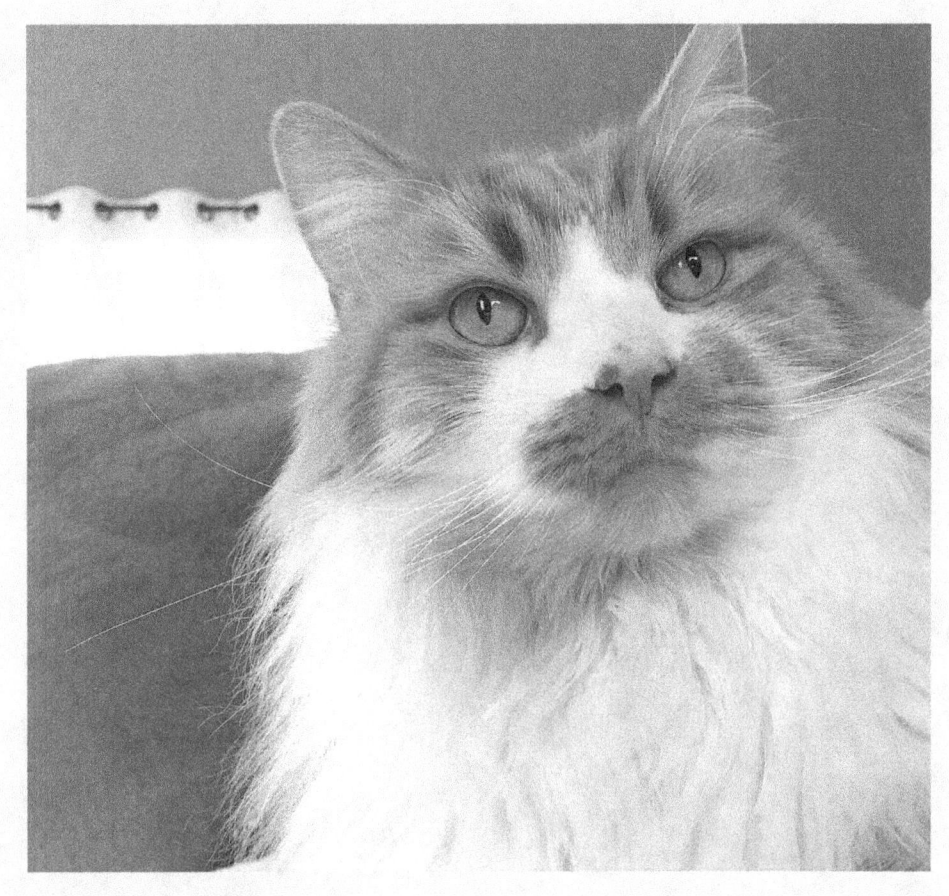
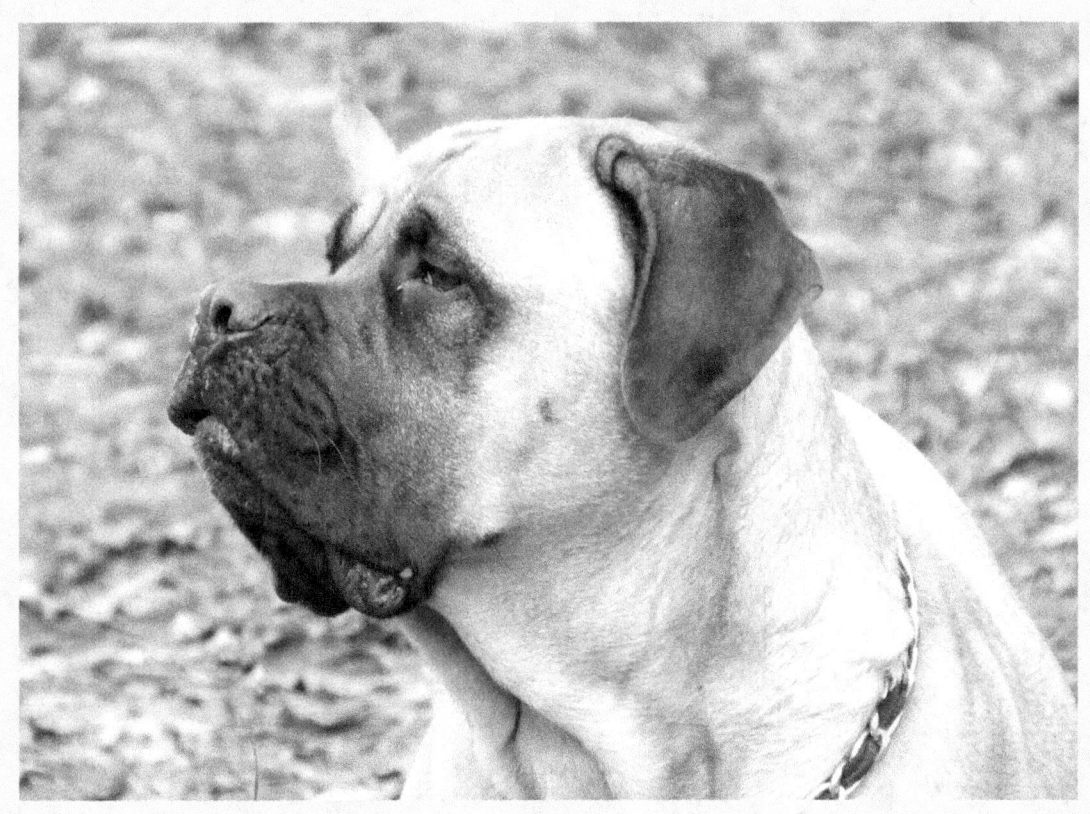

www.ingramcontent.com/pod-product-compliance
Lightning Source LLC
Chambersburg PA
CBHW062336220526
45469CB00008B/2734